OUR TOWN

50

TERRIFIC BAY AREA ESCAPES

BY GARY KAUF
WITH ROLAND DE WOLK

PHOTOGRAPHS BY JOHN SWAIN

CHRONICLE BOOKS
SAN FRANCISCO

Library of Congress Cataloging-in-Publication Data available.

Printed in Hong Kong.

ISBN 0-8118-0861-0

Cover photograph: Point Reyes Lighthouse; front flap photograph: Tilden; back cover: Marin County.
Cover calligraphy: Georgia Deaver
Photographs on page 4: Marin Headlands; page 5: Tomales.
Book design: Julie Noyes Long
Maps: Michael Carabetta and Anne Marie Milillo

Distributed in Canada by Raincoast Books,
8680 Cambie Street,
Vancouver, B.C. V6P 6M9

10 9 8 7 6 5 4 3 2 1

Chronicle Books
275 Fifth Street
San Francisco, CA 94103

TABLE OF CONTENTS

Introduction

⊞ ⊞ ⊞

There aren't many attractions left these days that won't cost you half a day's pay to enjoy. Taking in a baseball game can easily run a family of four $100; a couple of hours at the amusement park can be about the same; even going to a movie is no bargain. But this book is. *Our Town* offers fifty pleasant day outings, each within a reasonable driving range and each at a reasonable price. Pack a picnic lunch and pay for nothing but your gasoline. Stay a few hours, spend the day, or make it a mini-getaway weekend–it's up to you. Some of these places will remind you of the olden days or the Wild West, others are neighborhoods that have held onto their own unique flavor, and a few are just special places you might not have visited before. But each is guaranteed to provide a little slice of our gorgeous Bay Area that is off the heavily publicized–and heavily beaten–track. These are the hidden jewels of the Bay Area.

ABOUT *OUR TOWN*

Our Town was conceived in 1990 as a weekly television segment on the KTVU News program *Mornings on 2*. Over the past few years, we've traipsed all over Northern California in search of these special places. No town or locale paid for the privilege of being included in this book or the television series; in fact, in most cases, we never even

announced we were coming. We just showed up.

Our Town isn't meant to be a comprehensive guide to the Bay Area. In contrast to most travel books, which give you a few words about hundreds of places, we're out to give you a couple of hundred words about a few places, fifty to be exact. The pictures are meant to give you a feel for the place, the words–a taste of what you'll find and a base from which to start your exploration.

ABOUT THIS BOOK

As with any undertaking of this sort, many people have contributed enormous time and energy along the way. First on the list is my wife, Jayne Garrison, who provided me with encouragement and scores of quiet afternoons, so I could take these stories originally produced for the television and turn them into essay form. My sons, Alec and Chase, deserve thanks too for all those afternoons of playing with Dad that they, often unwillingly, gave up.

Then too, there are the cameramen who have been as much a part of *Our Town* as anyone, Sid Farhang and Chuck Leighton; videotape editors Dina Munsch and Ron Acker; and *Mornings on 2* Executive Producer Rosemarie Thomas, who gave the series time to develop—a great luxury in TV.

The idea of taking the television series and making it into a book came from Roland De Wolk, a friend and talented journalist in his own right. In fact, much of the writing, or should I say "rewriting," is his. Channel 2's Carol Conway and intern Bobbi McCulloch each spent hours hunting down videotapes, transcribing them, and checking facts. I am beholden as well to Judy Lewenthal, my editor at Chronicle Books, and her boss, Bill LeBlond, who gently and patiently led the way through this alien world of book publishing and introduced me to the work of John Swain, a photographer who possesses the magic to produce pictures far more powerful than any of my words.

That's it, I think, except for a last thank you to my college journalism teacher Sam Goldman. If it hadn't been for him, I would have majored in business administration.

GARY KAUF

1

San Francisco

chestnut street

CHESTNUT STREET IS ONE OF THE OLD-TIME STREETS OF SAN FRANCISCO. THERE'S A HEAVY ITALIAN INFLUENCE OUT HERE, AND A HEAVY EMPHASIS ON FOOD: ORIGINAL JOE'S, O'SOLE MIO, LUCCA DELI. LUCCA CLAIMS TO BE THE ONLY PLACE IN SAN FRANCISCO THAT STILL MAKES RAVIOLI BY HAND. WHATEVER THE CASE, EVERY WEDNESDAY YOU'LL FIND LOUIE DIGRANDE ROLLING OUT HIS DOUGH IN THE BACK, A HUGE VAT OF FILLING BOILING AWAY ON THE STOVE. LOUIE'S GOT IT DOWN TO A SCIENCE, RATHER THAN AN ART. HE SAYS IT TAKES YEARS TO DEVELOP JUST THE RIGHT TOUCH.

Making food fresh, and by hand seems to be a dying concept in our freeze-dried, vacuum-packed world — except on Chestnut Street. The merchants here believe a freshly roasted turkey breast will draw more customers than any sign. And that cheese carved right off the wheel makes better-tasting sandwiches somehow.

There is a particular flavor to this street that the people who work here are trying hard to hold onto — a neighborhood street flavor. Noah's Bagels, a bagel emporium that opened a couple of years ago, has been wildly successful in part because it has carried on that home-made tradition. Noah's counter people will tell you specifically which bagels are just out of the oven and still warm. And no matter what strange concoction you dream up, the answer is always yes.

Folks who live around here say they like the class of people on Chestnut Street: working class, no rowdies — all the people you would like in your neighborhood. And no one seems to care that there aren't *any* chestnut trees.

☞ **WHERE TO GO AND WHAT TO DO:**

LUCCA DELI, *2120 Chestnut Street. Ravioli-making on Wednesdays and Sundays between 7:00 am and noon. No tours, but if it's a slow Wednesday morning you can probably peek in the back.*

NOAH'S BAGELS, *2075 Chestnut Street. Noah's offers every variety of bagel you can think of — and some you haven't — and will smear just about anything on them. Grab your bagels and coffee and head for the Marina Green for a lovely lunch on the grass. Joggers, kite-flyers, and kids perform free every day here.*

PRESIDIO THEATRE, *1390 Chestnut Street. The Presidio is one of the last great old movie houses in San Francisco that hasn't been cut into mini-screens. Highly recommended.*

HOW TO GET THERE:

Chestnut is one block north of Lombard Street, the main route to the Golden Gate Bridge. The commercial stretch runs from Fillmore Street to Divisadero.

From the Peninsula:

Take the Bayshore Freeway into the city, then stay to the left and merge onto Highway 101. Exit almost immediately onto Van Ness Avenue and follow it north across town. Turn left at Lombard, right at Franklin, then left onto Chestnut, and follow it to the shopping area.

From the East Bay:

Cross the Bay Bridge, then take the Golden Gate Bridge exit (Highway 101). Follow the signs to Van Ness Avenue, and proceed as above.

south park

THERE IS A TINY NEIGHBORHOOD IN SAN FRANCISCO THAT EVEN MANY OF THE NATIVES DON'T KNOW ABOUT. IT'S CALLED SOUTH PARK, A TIGHT CLUSTER OF OLD HOMES AND APARTMENT BUILDINGS BUILT AROUND A LONG OVAL PARK. IT'S BORDERED BY BRYANT AND BRANNAN STREETS, BETWEEN 2ND AND 3RD. BUT THE ONLY WAY TO GET HERE IS UP A COUPLE OF OBSCURE SIDE STREETS AND ALLEYS. PEOPLE FIND IT BY ACCIDENT; THEN THEY CAN'T FIND IT AGAIN BECAUSE THEY DON'T KNOW HOW TO GET THERE.

Back in the 1800s, just before gold was discovered in California, South Park was one of the ritziest addresses in town. This is where the rich folks lived. It turned industrial in the 1940s and '50s, and seedy in the '60s. As seems to always happen in San Francisco though, when the neighborhood was at bottom investors and individuals moved in to rehabilitate the classic Victorian and Edwardian homes. Now South Park sports a couple of chic restaurants, the park is clean and green, and a lot of writers and artists are moving in.

South Park's attraction is that it's off the beaten track, which is a good trick in the city. No bus line runs through here, it's not a shortcut to anywhere, and there's nothing like it in the city — or the entire Bay Area for that matter. You might find something like this curving, tree-lined thoroughfare in old-town Boston or maybe Greenwich Village. South Park has kind of a European feel and an "alternative-lifestyle" quality. It's not swank Union Street or a bustling downtown.

And, there is another major advantage to living around here: South Park is perhaps 30 seconds from an on-ramp to the Bay Bridge. Parking is lousy, but living here sure cuts down on the commute.

It's a great place to walk your dog, too.

☞ **WHERE TO GO AND WHAT TO DO:**

RISTORANTE ECCO, *101 South Park.*

SOUTH PARK CAFE-RESTAURANT, *108 South Park.*

LUMBINI *(fancy gifts), 156 South Park.*

South Park is also within a couple of blocks of several of the best outlet stores.

HOW TO GET THERE:

From the Peninsula:

Take the Bayshore Freeway toward the Bay Bridge, and exit at 4th Street. This will put you onto Bryant Street. Turn right onto 2nd Street, then right into South Park.

From the East Bay:

Cross the Bay Bridge and, staying in the far left lane, exit at 5th Street. This will take you under the freeway, then make another left onto Bryant Street. Turn right at 2nd Street, then right into South Park.

mission rock

Y OU COULD SAY MISSION ROCK IS ON THE CRAGGY SIDE OF SAN FRANCISCO, ALONG THE NEGLECTED WATERFRONT SOUTH OF CHINA BASIN. THIS FORLORN AREA SEEMS ABOUT THE LAST PLACE YOU'D FIND A RESTAURANT, AND YOU HAVE TO WORK TO FIND THIS ONE. IT'S CALLED THE MISSION ROCK RESORT; NO ONE SEEMS TO KNOW WHERE THE "RESORT" PART COMES FROM, BUT THERE ARE TWO BARS AND AN OPEN-AIR PATIO-DECK RESTAURANT HERE. IT ISN'T DECORATED, THERE AREN'T ANY FERNS HANGING AROUND OR A LOT OF POLISHED BRASS — JUST SUN-BLEACHED WOOD TABLES, AND CHARCOAL-GRILLED HAMBURGERS FOR AROUND SIX BUCKS.

What's really special about this place though is the weather — and the view. There aren't that many places in San Francisco where you'd want to eat outdoors, but the weather here always seems to be good, or at least tolerable.

As for the view, it is, in a word, "gritty." A shipyard operates just across the marina so you can hear the dockworkers clanging away as you munch your lunch.

A couple of mornings a week a half dozen old-timers meet here for coffee. Many of them come back in the afternoon for a couple of beers. Some folks come and watch the birds or do a little fishing. Herring run pretty good some years. It's also a great place to just sit and think, a place with a lot of rocky charm.

☞ **WHERE TO GO AND WHAT TO DO:**

MISSION ROCK RESORT, *817 China Basin. Downstairs is pretty basic; there's a short-order cook and a bar. Upstairs is more interesting. An enclosed bar looks out over the marina. The outdoor restaurant-deck is also up here. Sailboats and a few working fishing vessels tie up here. Herring run in the winter months.*

THE RAMP, *855 China Basin. Just up the street from Mission Rock, this is a slightly upscale but still fairly rustic restaurant-bar.*

How to get there:

From San Francisco:

Take 3rd Street south. Make a left turn at Mission Rock Street, then turn right at China Basin Boulevard.

From the East Bay:

Cross the Bay Bridge and take the 5th Street exit. Head south (left) under the freeway and turn left at Bryant Street, then right onto 4th Street. Follow that to Rock Street and turn left, then turn right at China Basin Boulevard.

From the Peninsula:

Take 101 north to the 4th Street exit (the last San Francisco exit before the Bay Bridge), and make a right turn onto 4th Street. Follow that to Rock Street and turn left, then turn right at China Basin Boulevard.

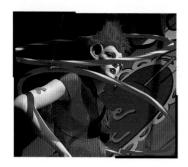

fillmore street

Thirty years ago Fillmore Street was considered the rough side of town: a little risqué, a little dangerous, a place you didn't go wandering around at night. But San Francisco has always been a city of change with neighborhoods moving up and down the economic and desirability scale. And Fillmore Street has been on a steady climb to where it's now well past "funky-chic."

The change became pronounced in the early 1970s. That's when the seedy bars and after-hours clubs were closed down. But the secondhand clothing stores stayed because this was a place where supply met demand. The haughty matrons from wealthy Pacific Heights would come here to dispose of the slightly used but outrageously expensive fashions they'd just bought last year, to be followed in the door by working-class Western Addition folks who were thrilled to buy up the designer labels at a fraction of their original cost. Eventually, the thrift stores began to attract enough attention that discount outlets began moving in. Then came the fashion boutiques, and all the new traffic on the street brought new restaurants.

Today, the still-reasonable rents have drawn a slew of furniture stores to the point where people come from all over the Bay Area to shop The Fillmore. The neighborhood has its own newspaper, and at night it's a major singles hangout with Harry's Bar, the Elite Cafe, and the Pacific Heights Bar and Grill (The "Pack-Bag"). You could say the Fillmore has come full circle now. From a wild street of party houses back then to one of the hippest streets in town.

☞ **WHERE TO GO AND WHAT TO DO:**

HARRY'S BAR, *2020 Fillmore Street.*

ELITE CAFE, *2049 Fillmore Street.*

PACIFIC HEIGHTS BAR AND GRILL, *2001 Fillmore Street.*

DEPARTURES FROM THE PAST *(thrift store), 2028 Fillmore Street.*

SAN FRANCISCO SYMPHONY THRIFT SHOP, *2223 Fillmore Street.*

How to get there:

From the Peninsula:

Take the Bayshore Freeway into San Francisco, then Highway 101 toward the Golden Gate Bridge. The freeway ends at Fell Street; follow it to Fillmore Street and turn right, then park around Bush or Pine Streets.

From the East Bay:

Take the Bay Bridge, then Highway 101 toward the Golden Gate Bridge. Proceed as above.

glen park

GLEN PARK IS NAMED FOR A NARROW, SECLUDED VALLEY ALMOST IN THE GEOGRAPHIC CENTER OF THE CITY; THE WELSH USED TO CALL THIS KIND OF PLACE A "GLYN". IN WET YEARS, A STREAM RUNS THROUGH THE PARK, QUICKLY DRYING UP BY SUMMER. IN FACT, SAN FRANCISCO USED TO HAVE A DOZEN STREAMS LIKE THIS, BUT THE REST HAVE BEEN COVERED OVER WITH CONCRETE.

Technically, the Glen Park neighborhood is an extension of the city's Mission District. What makes this place so identifiable, though, are its narrow, windy streets, weaving up the hill toward Diamond Heights, and suddenly hairpinning back the other way. If there is any one street in Glen Park that is completely level we couldn't find it.

But along with the small streets come small shops — coffee shops and markets instead of giant Safeways. The neighborhood seems to have been "overlooked" by the big chains. The key to Glen Park's character, however, is definitely its park, actually called Glen Canyon Park. Considering its location it seems relatively unspoiled, and the hiking trails are a wonderful antidote to too much civilization.

Local lore has it that outlaws used to hide out in Glen Canyon's caves. The canyon is so steep that the caves are almost impossible to find unless you know the way. Bootleggers are said to have used the caves as well to store their goods. Glen Park, it seems, was outside the law. And it's still a good place to get lost in.

☞ WHERE TO GO AND WHAT TO DO:

GLEN CANYON PARK. *The park itself stretches along O'Shaughnessy Boulevard from Portola at the top all the way down to Bosworth.*

Glen Park's main shopping area is on Chenery and Bosworth, but you'll find shops scattered about.

MT. DAVIDSON. *San Francisco's highest peak. A trail will take you to the 983-foot summit — and a gorgeous view of the Pacific if it isn't fogged in.*

How to get there:

From San Francisco:

Take Interstate 280, exit at Monterey Boulevard. Turn right at Circular Avenue, then left at Bosworth (near the BART station). Follow Bosworth up to the shopping district and park.

From the Peninsula:

Take Interstate 280 into San Francisco, exit at San Jose Avenue. Stay to the right and look for a tiny sign that says "Bosworth". Turn right, then follow the road past the BART station. Park wherever you can.

From the East Bay:

Take the Bay Bridge, then merge onto Interstate 280 south (toward the right). Exit at Monterey Boulevard. Turn right at Circular Avenue, then left at Bosworth (near the BART station). Follow Bosworth up to the shopping district and park.

old dutch

Driving along San Francisco's Ocean Beach you might catch a glimpse of some willowy wooden spars turning lazily in the breeze. "Old Dutch," the windmill is called — a musty stone monument to the days when only the winds and tide pushed water.

Old Dutch was built in 1902 to harness San Francisco's westerly winds and pump water into Golden Gate Park for badly needed irrigation. The chains and gears and drive shafts still turn today, but they don't push water anymore; it's all for show. An electric motor turns the windmill.

For decades around the middle of this century Old Dutch sat neglected and still. Then in the 1970s, a woman named Eleanor Rossi Crabtree spearheaded a drive to raise money to have it restored. In 1981 the sails turned once more. Not to pump water, of course, just to turn — our imagination.

Now people come and sit in the tulip garden beside the old windmill to look and daydream. "Chasing windmills," that used to be called, by people too busy to dream. It's a chance to see a bit of history, a piece of San Francisco from another time.

☞ WHERE TO GO AND WHAT TO DO:

Old Dutch is usually running but its maintenance schedule is erratic. You can call 415-753-7041 for information. The tulip garden is usually in full bloom in March.
As long as you're already in Golden Gate Park, consider these diversions:

STRYBING ARBORETUM, *along Martin Luther King Jr. Drive, east of the windmill. A flower lover's paradise with thousands of species of flowers, plants, and trees.*

BUFFALO PADDOCK, *along John F. Kennedy Drive at 36th Avenue. A small and somewhat lethargic herd of bison to look at while they look at you.*

SPRECKELS LAKE, *almost next to the Buffalo Paddock. Model enthusiasts use this large pond to test out their motorized miniature sailboats and such. The ducks and seagulls don't seem to mind.*

HOW TO GET THERE:

From San Francisco:

Take Lincoln Way to the west. Just before the park ends you can make a right turn onto South Drive. The windmill is a few hundred feet up the road.

From the Peninsula:

Take Interstate 280 north. It will lead you into San Francisco's 19th Avenue. The streets are alphabetical here, going in reverse order. Turn right at Irving Street, then take the next left, and left again onto Lincoln Way. Proceed as above.

From the East Bay:

Take the Bay Bridge, then get on Highway 101 and get off on Fell Street. Follow Fell Street into the park and it will eventually turn into Lincoln Way via Kezar Drive. Follow Lincoln Way until just before the park ends, then make a right turn onto South Drive. The windmill is just up the road.

the excelsior

THERE IS A LITTLE TOWN IN THE MIDDLE OF THE BIG TOWN THAT IS SAN FRANCISCO. IT'S A PLACE OFTEN HIDDEN BY THE FOG AND ALMOST ALWAYS FORGOTTEN BY THE TOUR BOOKS. *ABOVE SAN FRANCISCO, INSIDE SAN FRANCISCO,* YOU WON'T FIND A WORD ABOUT THE EXCELSIOR DISTRICT IN ANY OF THEM.

The word "Excelsior" means high or lofty, but this 10-by-12 block slice of the Mission District isn't either of those. The Excelsior used to be a neighborhood very popular with the working class "I's": Irish, Italians, the kind of folks who would just as soon buy you a drink as talk to you.

Louie Cosentino runs Alex's Place Cocktails. When someone asks him what nationality he is he'll say a hundred percent Excelsior. Louie says in the old days you could always spot someone from the neighborhood because they'd be the ones fighting to pay for a drink even though they were broke.

The streets in the Excelsior District are named for the world's major international capitals: London, Paris, Lisbon, etc. And if anything typifies the neighborhood these days it's the mix of color and culture. Next door to those Irish and Italians have moved Chinese, Taiwanese, Filipinos — everyone who wants a chance to make it in this country.

Phil Varelas took his shot. He opened the hofbrau-style restaurant Chick and Coop along Mission street. Phil likes to advertise Liver and Onions as his house special in a sign in the window. He says that dish is guaranteed to catch everyone's attention. Phil's other technique is to turn on the fan and vent his slow-cooked aromas outside.

The Excelsior's main shopping strip along Mission Street is only a couple of blocks long and the neighborhood is fairly compact, so everybody seems to know each other. That also makes it cozy, and to the folks who live here, comfortable. Their own little town.

☞ WHERE TO GO AND WHAT TO DO:

The heart of the neighborhood is the intersection of Mission Street and Ocean Avenue. A huge alfresco mural is painted on the side of a building announcing the place.

Sorrento Delicatessen, *4763 Mission Street; very good prices on very high-quality Italian goods.*

The Royal Baking Company, *next door to Sorrento's. One of the last places to get handmade grissini, the authentic Italian bread stick.*

Chick And Coop Restaurant, *4500 Mission Street; hofbrau-style food prepared fresh daily.*

How to get there:

From San Francisco:
Take Interstate 280 south to the Mission/Alemany exit. Turn left, then make another left at Mission Street to Ocean Avenue.

From the Peninsula:
Take Interstate 280 north to the Ocean Avenue exit and follow Ocean Avenue to Mission Street.

From the East Bay:
Take the Bay Bridge into San Francisco, then take Interstate 280 south to the Mission/Alemany exit. Turn left, then make another left at Mission Street to Ocean Avenue.

potrero hill

Potrero Hill used to be considered "the other side" of San Francisco, "the industrial section." Then folks discovered the great views and the sunshine. Potrero Hill is smack in the middle of San Francisco's narrow and elusive sun belt. If it's sunny anywhere, it'll be here first.

The center of the neighborhood is a commercial strip along 18th and Missouri streets. There are coffee shops and restaurants, bookstores and a bar, Bloom's Saloon. Bloom's has preserved some of the city's rough-hewn character from its unvarnished days. The saloon isn't fancy, but it offers a one-of-a-kind back door view of the city's downtown and is loaded with political and sports memorabilia. One more thing: the drinks are cheap.

Farley's, a 1950s-style coffee house, is right across the street. This is the kind of coffee house that's made for long, lazy Sunday mornings with the *New York Times*. Farley's has its own fairly comprehensive magazine rack along one wall. But why read when you can just sip and study the society. Potrero Hill draws artists, new-wave musicians, overage beatniks, and hippy handymen.

People like to live on this hill because the rents are a little cheaper, parking is a little easier, and the mood, like the temperature, is a little warmer. It's a comfortable slice of the city's diversity. One of San Francisco's former mayors lived here for years, and now comes back frequently for lunch at Klein's Deli at 20th and Connecticut. He says it's the only place in the city where you can take a sandwich and eat it outside — without freezing.

☞ **Where to go and what to do:**

Bloom's Saloon, *1318 18th Street. Good San Francisco bar, great view.*

Farley's, *1315 18th Street.*

Bottom of the hill bar and restaurant, *1233 17th Street.*

Garibaldi's Cafe, *1600 17th Street. The restaurant specializes in wonderful fish dishes. It also has a takeout window along the side.*

Check out the bar that connects to Garibaldi's. It's a dive, but one with a ton of personality.

All the tourist books say Lombard Street is "the crookedest street in the world," but it's not. Vermont Street, on the back side of Potrero Hill, is. It begins at 22nd and Vermont and hairpins all the way down the hill to Army Street.

POTRERO GARDENS, *17th and Texas streets. One of the friendlier nurseries around, and one that specializes in hard to find vegetables such as organic tomato starters and orange and yellow cherry tomato starters.*

HOW TO GET THERE:

From San Francisco:
The heart of the neighborhood is 18th and Missouri streets. The easiest way to get there is to take 16th Street all the way to Missouri, turn right, and park around 18th Street.

From the Peninsula:
Take the Bayshore Freeway into San Francisco and exit at Vermont Street. Go straight through the intersection and continue on to Missouri Street. Park as close to 18th Street as you can.

From the East Bay:
Take the Bay Bridge into San Francisco. Exit at the 8th Street ramp and stay in the leftmost lane. This will put you on 8th Street heading south. Follow 8th Street as it goes under the freeway and then curves around a bit. Turn left at 16th Street, then right onto Missouri, and follow it up to 18th Street.

columbus avenue

THE SIZZLE IS GONE FROM SAN FRANCISCO'S BAWDY BROADWAY, BUT THERE'S A DIS-TINCTIVE AROMA STILL STRONG ALONG COLUMBUS AVENUE. IT'S A THICK, PUNGENT, SPICY SMELL, HEAVY ON THE SALAMI AND CHEESE. MUST BE NORTH BEACH.

Italians will tell you that food is central to their culture. Molinari Delicatessen on Columbus and Vallejo is doing everything it can to validate that theory. The place is jam-packed with prosciuttos and pastas and peppers. And salami. Many, many salamis: Soprasetta, Toscano, Garlic, Genoa, Copa Veneziana. You get the idea.

What Molinari's does with the spicy stuff a little place just down the street called Mara's Italian Pastries does with the sweet. Owner Gino Torrano gets up around three in the morn-ing, every morning, to whip up his authentic Italian delicacies: napoleon, zuppa inglese, canoli. Smell, presentation, and reputation are all-important along this street.

The old-world charm of the neighborhood may be typified by a place with the quirky name of Mario's Bohemian Cigar Store Cafe. Mario's looks out on Washington Square, where Columbus and Union Street meet. And the clientele is as curious as the building itself. There is a real "Mario" by the way, but he always seems to be out playing Bocce Ball.

Across Broadway there are a couple more special spots. One is Vesuvio Cafe at 255 Columbus. Vesuvio's was a hangout for the beatnik crowd in the 50s. From the windows upstairs you can sip cappuccino and watch the street parade below.

Next door to Vesuvio's is another North Beach landmark: City Lights Bookstore. Poets Lawrence Ferlinghetti, Allen Ginsberg, and Jack Kerouac used to hang out in these jumbled, rambling rooms. You'll still find chairs, stools, and an occasional ottoman strewn about for those who want to taste before they buy.

☞ **WHERE TO GO AND WHAT TO DO:**

MOLINARI DELICATESSEN, *373 Columbus Avenue at Vallejo.*

MARA'S ITALIAN PASTRIES, *503 Columbus Avenue.*

MARIO'S BOHEMIAN CIGAR STORE CAFE, *566 Columbus Avenue.*

POSTERMAT, *401 Columbus Avenue. This place carries an extensive collection of original and reprinted rock'n'roll posters. You might call it "a blast from the past."*

VESUVIO CAFE, *255 Columbus Avenue (south of Broadway).*

CITY LIGHTS BOOKSTORE, *261 Columbus Avenue (south of Broadway).*

CAFE TRIESTE, *Vallejo and Grant. The perfect place to go for an espresso nightcap if you don't mind opera music blasting away over your conversation.*

HOW TO GET THERE:

From San Francisco:
Take Van Ness Avenue all the way to Broadway, then go east and follow Broadway to Columbus. It's the big intersection where Columbus crosses at an angle. Park wherever you can — it's tough here.

From the Peninsula:
Take the Bayshore Freeway into San Francisco, then take the Golden Gate Bridge (Highway 101) turnoff. Exit immediately, then turn right at the bottom of the ramp onto Mission Street, then left onto Van Ness Avenue and proceed as above.

From the East Bay:
Take the Bay Bridge into San Francisco, then take the Golden Gate Bridge (Highway 101) turnoff. Proceed as above.

south beach

Nestled in the shadows of the anchorage of the San Francisco–Oakland Bay Bridge, life is thriving once again in a forgotten neighborhood called South Beach. For decades, seagulls ruled this roost. The area was filled with vacant anonymous warehouses, a strip of rotting harbor, and a creosote-soaked pier. On weekends it was totally deserted. About the only draw left was Red's Java House, an old-fashioned diner with old-fashioned prices. The diner predates the Bay Bridge. And it may be the last place in the city where you can buy a burger and a beer for $2.35. A longshoreman lunch, they call it.

Red's Java House still has the blue-collar crowd, but the suit and tie set is also coming down this way now. They go across the Embarcadero to the Delancey Street Restaurant for their cheeseburger with blue cheese or swiss Gruyére: $5.50 plus tip.

Ten steps from there is the trendy Embarko run by the colorful and outspoken Joe Leis. Embarko opened its doors when this area was still mostly architects' plans and mud. It survived the earthquake of 1989, and the demolition of the Embarcadero Freeway in 1991 and 1992, but almost didn't survive the city's project to beautify the Embarcadero and run a streetcar line down here.

The draw of this neighborhood is that it's downtown living without the density; most of the condo developments are no more than three stories tall and there's still a lot of open space. Then of course it's very convenient, it's near the water, and the weather is about as good as you'll get. A pleasant and uncrowded setting to eat lunch, walk a little, and think. While the rest of the world passes by on the gargantuan concrete and iron of the Bay Bridge overhead.

☞ WHERE TO GO AND WHAT TO DO:

RED'S JAVA HOUSE, *Embarcadero and Bryant, right on the Bay. This place is just burgers and very basic.*

JAVA HOUSE. *A quarter-mile farther south on the Embarcadero, this Java House has no connection to the other and offers a more traditional-style breakfast and lunch. Not fancy, but the food is well-prepared.*

SFFD Firehouse #35. *This is where the San Francisco Fire Department keeps its fireboat* Phoenix. *Walk around the side and you may see firefighters polishing her up.*

Embarko and Delancey Street Restaurant. *Two fancy and tasty restaurants sit across from one another at Brannan and Embarcadero.*

Another option: Hit the quick and cheap deli at Mission and Beale called Brendan's for a couple of bag lunches, then park along the Embarcadero near Bryant Street and stroll along the Bay until you find a pleasant spot to sit and eat. On sunny days this is a real San Francisco treat.

How to get there:

From San Francisco:
Take the Embarcadero to Harrison Street or follow Harrison Street down to the Embarcadero.

From the Peninsula:
Take the Bayshore Freeway to the 4th Street exit. It will deposit you on Bryant Street. Stay on Bryant all the way to the Embarcadero.

From the East bay:
Take the Bay Bridge, and take the very first exit on your left as you enter the city. It will loop around and under the bridge. Then make a right at the first intersection and follow the road down to the Embarcadero.

❈　❈　❈

hayes valley

T HE BIG EARTHQUAKE OF 1989 MAY HAVE BEEN THE BEST THING TO EVER HAPPEN TO A NEIGH-
BORHOOD CALLED HAYES VALLEY. BEFORE THE BIG JOLT, A FREEWAY CUT THROUGH THIS PART OF
THE CITY. AFTER THE QUAKE, DAMAGE WAS SO SEVERE THAT ENGINEERS DECIDED TO DEMOLISH A
SECTION OF THE DOUBLE-DECKER FREEWAY — THE SECTION THAT CUT RIGHT THROUGH HAYES
VALLEY.

The difference, once the concrete and rubble were gone, was phenomenal. The freeway,
running diagonally through eight blocks of the Hayes Valley neighborhood, had become a
kind of demarcation line, and the darkness underneath the columns a no-man's-land. Take
away the freeway, and its noise and soot and general ugliness, and replace it with calm and
sunlight and eucalyptus trees, and you instantly create neighborhood pride.

Along with the venerable Hayes Street Grill, there is a definite ethnic flavor developing
here. A Chicago-style deli and a Middle-Eastern cafe have opened up, along with galleries and
shops. A delicatessen with the unorthodox name Moishe's Pippic draws transplanted New
Yorkers and the City Hall crowd. That's because at about 10:30 every morning owner Joe
Sattler starts slicing his fresh-out-of-the-oven hot pastrami, extra-lean, on fresh rye. They say
it's the best you'll find this side of New York's Carnegie Deli. Who are we to argue?

And, in case you're curious, "Moishe's Pippic" is Yiddish for "Moishe's bellybutton."

☞ **WHERE TO GO AND WHAT TO DO:**

HAYES STREET GRILL, *320 Hayes Street.*

MOISHE'S PIPPIC, *425 Hayes Street.*

WORLDWARE, *336 Hayes Street. Features politically correct clothing and
furniture; all natural materials.*

KIMBALL'S RESTAURANT, *300 Grove Street. One of the few jazz venues left
in the Bay Area. Call 415-861-5555 for show times.*

How to get there:

From the East Bay:

Take the Bay Bridge into San Francisco, then take the Golden Gate Bridge (Highway 101) turnoff. Exit immediately, then turn right at the bottom of the ramp onto Mission Street, then left onto Van Ness Avenue. Turn left on Hayes Street. The neighborhood begins after two blocks.

From the Peninsula:

Take the Bayshore Freeway into San Francisco and proceed as above.

the cliff house

To take a stroll into San Francisco's rich and colorful past, head for the rocks just to the north of Ocean Beach. Point Lobos, the area is technically called, but most natives know it as The Cliff House. This craggy point isn't the hot spot of the city as it was early in the century when George Whitney had his grand castle here, and Adolph Sutro his elegant and very popular Sutro Baths, but a little of the feel of old San Francisco survives: the crashing surf, the seal rocks (though the sea lions have all moved to Pier 39), and a little museum that is easy to miss — The Musée Mécanique.

In fact, the Musée Mécanique has been here for 90 years. Inside its damp and salty basement quarters are perhaps one million dollars worth of restored and fully operational amusement devices. Not electronic games, but the old, mechanical type. Like World Series Baseball, made by Rockola in 1927. A pitcher rears back and hurls a little steel ball for hitters to swing at using a metal lever connected to a bat. The umpire even calls balls and strikes.

Just across from the baseball machine sits the Gumball Crane. See how many gumballs you can scoop up and drop into a hopper in a minute and a half. There's Peppy the Dancing Clown; a silent-movie picture machine circa 1900 offering Marilyn Monroe in a variety of sexy poses; The Hammer (see if you've got the strength to ring the bell); and the museum's mascot, "Laughing Sal," a bawdy old gal who used to be in the Fun House at the now long gone Playland-at-the-Beach. Sixty seconds worth of her raucous laughter is plenty.

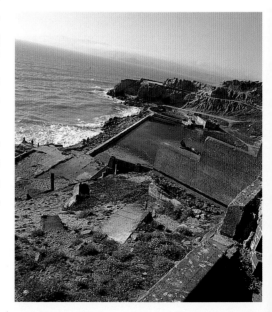

When you tire of the games or run out of coins, spend a moment looking at the old black-and-white and sepia-tone photos covering the museum's walls: the baths, Playland, the Fun House, the rickety roller coaster.

About the only thing that has survived, besides "Laughing Sal," is the "It's It" Ice Cream sandwich, which was invented at Playland. The original concoction was fairly simple: a huge slab of vanilla ice cream put between two oatmeal cookies and dipped in chocolate. After Playland closed "It's It" disappeared for awhile. Now its back in a number of different flavors, and packaged to last forever. But still pretty tasty.

☞ WHERE TO GO AND WHAT TO DO:

THE CLIFF HOUSE. *This sprawling complex now offers extravagant and somewhat pricey breakfasts upstairs, seafood and shellfish lunches and dinners in the main dining room, and drinks at the bar. Ask for a window table and watch the fog come in.*

MUSÉE MÉCANIQUE. *Downstairs from the Cliff House; either concrete stairway will get you there. It's open 11:00 am to 7:00 pm Monday through Friday; 10:00 am to 8:00 pm weekends and holidays.*

SUTRO BATHS. *Thirty feet north of the Cliff House, notice the waves crashing over chunks of concrete. This was the old Sutro Baths, destroyed by fire in 1966. The baths were constructed so the rising and falling tide would circulate through, keeping the pools filled and clean.*

LAND'S END. *This is the bitter end of San Francisco, and many an amateur explorer has lost his life climbing around on the treacherous rocks. They are tempting, but don't. Stick to the walking paths, and take in the gorgeous view.*

How to get there:

From San Francisco:

Take Geary Boulevard all the way to the ocean, or take Sloat Boulevard, then right on Great Highway.

From the Peninsula:

Take Interstate 280 into the city; it will become 19th Avenue. At Irving Street make a right turn, then a left at the next block, then another left to get onto Lincoln Way. Follow Lincoln to the end and turn right on to the Great Highway. The Cliff House will be just up the hill.

From the East Bay:

After crossing the Bay Bridge take Highway 101 toward the Golden Gate Bridge. The last off-ramp is Fell Street; follow it through Golden Gate park and it becomes Lincoln Way. Follow Lincoln to the end and turn right on to the Great Highway. The Cliff House is a quarter-mile up the hill.

hyde street pier

ONCE UPON A TIME, REALLY NOT SO LONG AGO, SAN FRANCISCO WAS A SEAFARING TOWN, A PLACE AWASH WITH BIG WOODEN SHIPS, SALTY SAILORS, AND TALES OF THE HIGH SEAS. THESE DAYS, ABOUT THE ONLY SALT THAT'S LEFT IS IN THE AIR. AS FOR SHIPS, YOU MIGHT HEAD FOR THE HYDE STREET PIER AT THE FOOT OF HYDE STREET NEAR GHIRARDELLI SQUARE. HERE YOU CAN CLIMB ABOARD AND CRAWL AROUND THE FULL-RIGGED CAPE HORN SAILING SHIP, *THE BALCLUTHA,* BUILT IN 1886; OR SHIVER THE TIMBERS OF THE THREE-MASTED SCHOONER, THE *C.A. THAYER.*

The Hyde Street Pier was built in 1922 as a terminal for the Golden Gate Ferry running to Sausalito. *The Balclutha* never actually tied up here, but it called in San Francisco with its load of coal and cargo, taking with her California-grown grain for the trip around Cape Horn (or "Cape Stiff" as that isolated, wind-blasted thumb of land was once called by the poor jacks who had to make the arduous journey).

In 1986 *The Balclutha,* the *Thayer,* a steam-paddle ferry called *The Eureka,* and the schooner *Alma* (which used to work the Sacramento Delta) were brought here to be fixed up and put on display so the public could get a taste of America's seafaring past. The boats are still being fixed up, and the Hyde Street Pier's mission, as defined by the San Francisco Maritime Historical Park, which oversees it, has been expanded. Now, student groups frequently come down for a bit of hands-on learning and a relatively painless lesson in history. Sailing instructor Micah Faust-Allnutt often dresses up as Captain Ahab and puts the children through a list of shipboard chores, bringing a little physics and math into the mix. Makes the schoolwork a lot more interesting.

One young man effusively told us all he'd just learned about hoisting the sails and battening a hatch. "Actually being on board and knowing what it was like," he bubbled, "this is much better than TV."

A living museum on San Francisco Bay.

HYDE STREET PIER. *Open 10:00 am - 6:00 pm summer months; 9:30 am - 5:00 pm winter months. Admission $3 adults, $1 juniors. An Environmental Living Program is offered for children in which they get to stay overnight on one of the ships.*

HOW TO GET THERE:

From San Francisco:

Take Van Ness Avenue north. Right at North Point, left at Hyde. Parking is tough, but there are a couple of lots.

From the East Bay:

Bay Bridge to Bayshore Freeway. Then take the Golden Gate Bridge (Highway 101) turnoff. Exit immediately, then turn right at the bottom of the ramp onto Mission Street, then left onto Van Ness Avenue and follow Van Ness all the way to North Point. Turn right, then left on Hyde.

From the Peninsula:

Take the Bayshore Freeway into the city, then take the Golden Gate Bridge (Highway 101) turnoff. Exit immediately, then turn right at the bottom of the ramp onto Mission Street, then left onto Van Ness Avenue and proceed as above.

▣ ▣ ▣

treasure island

THERE WAS A TIME WHEN TREASURE ISLAND — THE FLAT, NEARLY SQUARE, MAN-MADE PATCH OF LAND IN THE MIDDLE OF SAN FRANCISCO BAY — WAS ON ITS WAY TO BECOMING THE BIG AIRPORT FOR THE BAY AREA. IN FACT, THE OLD CHINA CLIPPERS USED TO BEGIN THEIR TREK TO THE FAR EAST BY TAXIING OUT FROM THE SANDY SHOALS NEXT TO YERBA BUENA ISLAND AND LIFTING OFF ABOVE THE GOLDEN GATE — PAN AMERICAN AIRWAYS FLIGHT 001.

In the early 1930s San Francisco wanted to use this spot to host a world's fair in celebration of the building of the Golden Gate and Bay bridges. Civic leaders asked the federal government for money to fill in the shoals and make a new island. They were told that the government didn't build fairgrounds, only dams, parks, airports, that sort of thing. So the city fathers said, "Oh yes, by the way, when the fair is over we're going to turn it into an international airport. We've already got an airline landing there." They got the money.

The International Exposition on Treasure Island was a spectacular success, with tourists and locals flocking to this magical spot shimmering on San Francisco Bay. A great place for a fair, but a lousy place for an airport as it turned out. The runways would be too short, and the bridges would be a hazard to planes. Eventually the navy made a deal with the city to take over the land, turning it into a naval station. Now, the naval station is being decommissioned, and no one is quite sure what to do with the place. It's picturesque, with views of the city, the Golden Gate, the East Bay; but it's also windy and cold, and the ocean salt eats away at the base housing.

Whatever happens to the base, however, the Treasure Island Museum will probably remain, and it is a treasure not to be missed. The museum is in one of Pan Am's old hangars, and is chock-full of memorabilia from the fair, including 25-foot-tall art deco statues, as well as curiosities from Pan Am's early days. A wonderful place to visit, but you probably wouldn't want to live here.

☞ **WHERE TO GO AND WHAT TO DO:**

TREASURE ISLAND MUSEUM, *open 10:00am - 3:00pm every day. $2 donation.*

HOW TO GET THERE:

From San Francisco and the Peninsula:

Take the Bay Bridge and exit at Treasure Island. The museum is just inside the gates of the naval station.

From the East Bay:

Take the Bay Bridge and stay in the left lane for the Yerba Buena Island exit. It loops around, and signs will direct you to Treasure Island. The museum is just inside the gates of the naval station.

2

The Peninsula

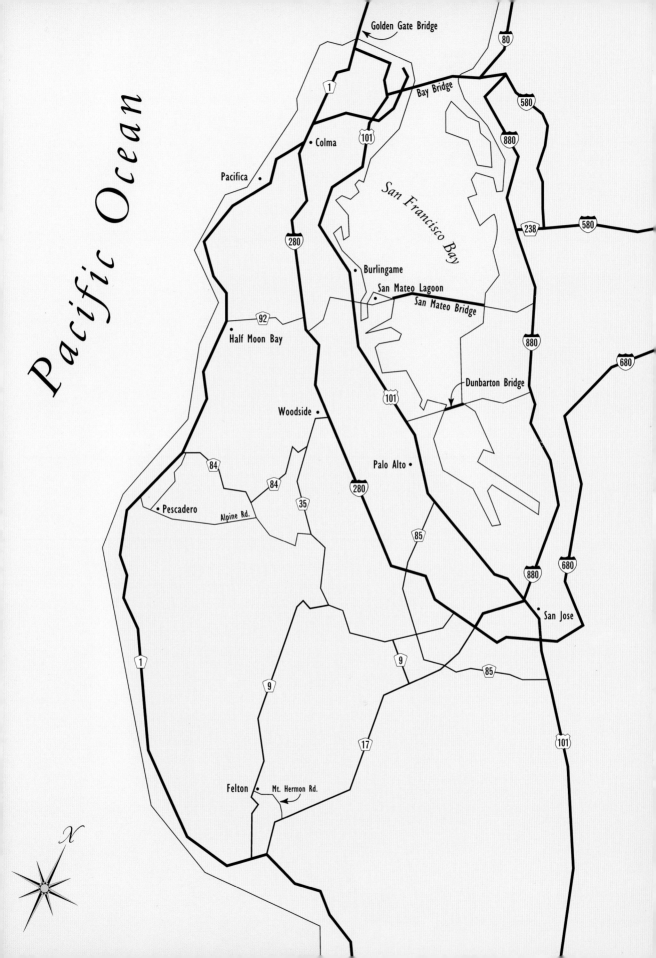

colma

Colma, California. Population 1,142 living; and a million-and-a-half other souls. Buried in these hills are the wealthy, the powerful, the infamous: Wild West lawman Wyatt Earp, a simple stone slab marking his grave; jazz great Turk Murphy, his tombstone carrying the cryptic inscription "little enough." Clothing manufacturer Levi Strauss is buried here in a great stone tomb. So are newspaper barons William Randolph Hearst and *San Francisco Chronicle* co-founder Charles de Young. Emperor Norton, a colorful San Francisco resident who once proclaimed himself imperial ruler of the city, is ensconced at Holy Cross Cemetery; Ishi, the "last native Californian" is at Olivet Memorial Park. Some of these shrines are great granite temples in the half-million dollar range. One recent big spender put $1.8 million into his mausoleum.

The shrines alone are worth the trip, but the grounds are also sure to astonish. City boosters know this and have a little brochure they put out that says "this city is in many ways superior to most parks throughout the country."

You might also want to stop by the Pet Cemetery featuring, among other celebrity canines, the final resting place of singer Tina Turner's dog.

Colma residents cheerfully call their town a necropolis: a city of the dead. Until 1941 the town's name was Lawndale — for obvious reasons. The post office ordered a name change because there was a Lawndale near Los Angeles. And that was that.

For those who need a bracer before touring Colma's particular pleasures, we suggest a stop at Malloy's Tavern, the sprawling, century-old bar right in the center of town along Mission Road. It always has at least a couple of regulars hanging about who love to surprise and regale visitors with their stock of Colma jokes, such as "People are just dying to get here." They will also claim, with a straight face, that the town motto is "It's great to be alive in Colma." On your way out notice the ornate entryway. It looks very much like it was designed to accommodate a hearse.

In fact, as you get to know Colma, you'll find it's anything but a sleepy little cemetery town. What it is is a blue-collar, Irish-Italian community nestled in a narrow slice of land between San Francisco and the overbearing San Bruno Mountains. Colma is just five minutes away from the big city, but here residents boast that they usually leave the keys in the ignition of their four-wheel drives, rarely bother locking the door, and don't fret about letting their children walk home by themselves from school.

And, there is one benefit to living in Colma that, to our knowledge, no other Bay Area community offers: free sports tickets. Each year the city of Colma offers its residents tickets to San Francisco Giants baseball games; free 49er football tickets; and ducats to see the Golden State Warriors basketball team play. The town doesn't have its own recreation department, so it uses that part of the budget to buy the season tickets. Colma has the money because of all the sales tax revenue coming in from the 280 Metro Center, its very popular factory outlet complex. Little Colma also has its own Auto Row.

Except for the weather, which is perpetual fog, the people who are alive in Colma say it's a great place to live. And besides, they say with a slight smirk, "Sooner or later anyone who's anyone in San Francisco — ends up here."

☞ WHERE TO GO AND WHAT TO DO:

MALLOY'S TAVERN, *1655 Mission Road, South San Francisco. An old-fashioned bar filled with town memorabilia and regulars who love to talk.*

Pick up a copy of the Cemetery Guide at Colma Town Hall, 1198 El Camino Real. 415-997-8300. The guide will tell you how to get to the graves of the rich and famous. It costs $2.50. Cypress Lawn is a must; you'll also find Japanese, Jewish, Christian, Serbian, and Greek cemeteries, and one exclusively for pets.

280 METRO CENTER. *This factory outlet center is for adults, but you can take the kids to the Discovery Zone, an indoor recreation facility across the parking lot.*

ROD MCLELLAN ORCHIDS. *About half a mile down Mission Boulevard in neighboring South San Francisco is a tropical wonderland. McLellan's offers free tours of its acres of orchids. The area's damp, foggy climate is ideal for growing many of the world's most exotic plants.*

From San Francisco:

Take Interstate 280 south to the Serramonte Boulevard exit. Turn left and go all the way to El Camino Real. The cemeteries are to the left, to the right, and directly in front of you.

From the Peninsula:

Take Interstate 280 north to the Hickey Boulevard exit. Turn right and go all the way to El Camino Real. Cemetery row is to the left.

From the East Bay:

Take the Bay Bridge into the city, then take Interstate 280 south to the Serramonte Boulevard exit. Turn left and go all the way to El Camino Real. The cemeteries are right there.

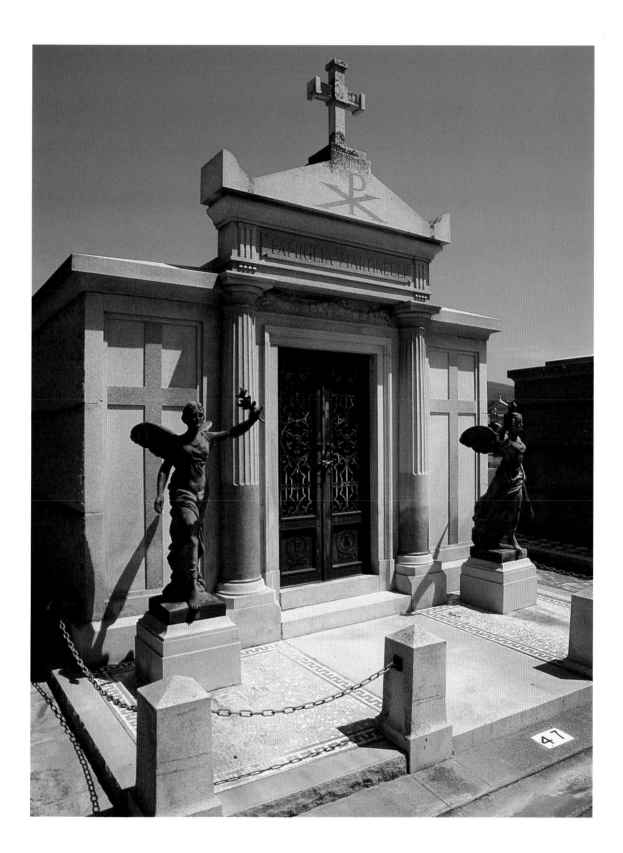

burlingame

THE TOWN OF BURLINGAME CALLS ITSELF "THE CITY OF TREES." AND THERE IS AN EXTRAORDI-
NARY ARRAY OF GREEN HERE: MULTICOLORED MAPLES AND STATELY OAKS, WHITE-FLOWERING
ELDERS, AND WIRY POPLARS. MANY OF THESE TREES HAVE BEEN PRUNED OVER DECADES TO CRE-
ATE GRACEFUL CANOPIES ABOVE THE STREETS. THE EFFECT IS A WARM, LUSH FEEL AS YOU DRIVE
ALONG — AND TO MAKE YOU WANT TO DRIVE A LITTLE SLOWER AND ADMIRE THE FINE VIEW. AND
THAT'S JUST WHAT THE PEOPLE WHO LIVE IN THIS TOWN SEEM TO HAVE IN MIND.

Burlingame is a slower-paced place that isn't really trying to keep up with the times. The
barber shop still has the revolving pole outside. And it smells like barber shops used to with
that powerful scent of Brylcreem coming from inside. The owner, Clyde Almond, still strops
his straight-edge razor before giving a shave and makes sure the cream is steaming hot. And
then you have to allow a certain amount of extra time for "snip and chat."

Then there's Preston's Candies along Broadway, an olden-times candy shop with its own
little Willie Wonka in the back. He's 75-year-old Art Preston. Just about every Thursday
morning you'll find Art racing around in back creating his sweet delights: chocolate fudge and
chocolate caramels, nougats and soft-centers and caramel corn. Art credits his longevity to
eating at least one piece of chocolate every day.

Burlingame was named after the honorable Anson Burlingame, President Abraham
Lincoln's minister to China. According to local lore, Burlingame came here to visit in the
early 1860s and fell in love with the oak-clad rolling hills. So he bought a thousand acres to
build a villa.

Today, 27,000 people live in this homey little place. Residents call it quaint and rustic.
They say it feels a lot like one of those small towns in the Midwest. There isn't any place for
Burlingame to grow; they control the traffic and the parking. So everything remains fairly
comfortable — the living, a little easier.

☞ WHERE TO GO AND WHAT TO DO:

*CalTrain is a great way to get here. Trains stop at 290 California Street, right at Burlingame Avenue, the main
drag that boasts lots of quaint retail shops.*

PRESTON'S CANDIES, *1170 Broadway. Candy making on Thursdays beginning at 9:30 am. Viewing by appointment. Call 415-344-3254.*

KOHN MANSION *(also known as "The Oaks"), 2750 Adeline Drive. This 19th-century mansion was built as a summer home for Frederick Kohn, a prominent San Franciscan of the time. The land now belongs to the Sisters of Mercy and is part of the campus of Mercy High School. The mansion is rented out for special events.*

HOW TO GET THERE:

From San Francisco and the Peninsula:
Take Highway 101 to the Burlingame exit.

From the East Bay:
Take the San Mateo Bridge (Highway 92), then head north on Highway 101 to the Burlingame exit.

pescadero

Off the twisting and well-traveled coastal highway, better known as Highway 1, is the Town of Pescadero, a little spot that feels as if it's been lost in time. The name means "fish town" in Portuguese, and back in the last century whales were also hunted as they migrated north through the waters off these shores.

Today, this part of southern San Mateo County is primarily farmland. Artichokes grow particularly well in Pescadero's damp coastal climate. There is also a lot of land available for grazing. Horse trainers and breeders say the wide-open ranges and miles of beach make Pescadero perfect horse country.

Most of Pescadero is owned by a handful of well-off families, among them, the Duarte family. They still operate the stylish old Italian-Portuguese restaurant in the middle of town. Owning the land gives the Duartes and the other families a fair amount of control over the town, but it's a benevolent sort of control. For example, no billboards or advertising clutter are allowed within Pescadero's city limits. Apartment rents are kept low, and new construction is rare. The families seem to feel it's their duty to take care of things on what they call their side of the hill.

The "hill" is the small mountain range that separates Pescadero from the bigger cities of San Mateo, Burlingame, and Redwood City, where the county government has a lot more control. Little Pescadero, by contrast, is an isolated, one-lane, one-road, single-story town. The schoolhouse isn't exactly the fabled one-room kind with barefoot boys and severe schoolmarms, but you can still find cattle nibbling on a grassy hillside directly behind the school yard.

Residents say living in a place like Pescadero makes them feel calmer and more secure. Visitors feel that slower, gentler pace, too. The folks who live here know they've got something special: ocean on one side, green hills on the other. And coming into town along Highway 1, a beautiful stretch of rocky beach rivals any other in Northern California. Pescadero — a little town with a funny name that's a lot of fun to spend a day in.

☞ WHERE TO GO AND WHAT TO DO:

ARTICHOKES. *Duarte's Tavern for artichoke soup and fresh French bread. For fried artichokes served year-round, try Tony's Restaurant, right across the street.*

NORM'S MARKET, *along Stage Road (the main street through town). Outstanding fresh-baked bread seven days a week. Garlic and Herb bread is the biggest seller, followed by artichoke.*

PHIPP'S RANCH, *along Highway 84 just east of town. Phipp's Ranch offers pick-your-own strawberries, blackberries, and raspberries. They'll remind you of what really fresh fruit tastes like. The season runs from June to October. Kids will love the barnyard area with old farm machinery to climb on and pony rides on the weekends.*

PIGEON POINT LIGHTHOUSE. *This youth hostel along Highway 1 is a cheap, clean, and scenic place to spend the night and it's not just for backpack-toting students. Lots of well-scrubbed, middle-class families are discovering California's hostels and you'll have a bit of an adventure for the kids. Call ahead for reservations and be sure to check out the outdoor hot tub. What a view!*

HOW TO GET THERE:

From San Francisco:

Take Highway 1 south approximately 30 miles.

From the Peninsula:

Take Interstate 280 north to Highway 92 west. Follow it to Highway 1, and then go south about 15 miles.

From the East Bay:

Take the San Mateo Bridge (Highway 92), and follow it through the mountains to Highway 1, then go south about 15 miles.

✽ ✽ ✽

woodside

Driving into the town of Woodside along Highway 84, the first thing that catches your eye is a whitewashed building that looks to be right out of "Gunsmoke." This was once the Pioneer Hotel and Saloon. There's still a small bar downstairs, but now the building is mostly offices. It's just that no one sees any reason to change the nostalgic old facade.

Woodside is a real casual town, a horse town. It's still very rural; the big debate in town is whether they should put in sidewalks. But it's not as though they can't afford them. Woodside is one of the Bay Area's most affluent communities.

Woodside came into being as a lumber town in the past century. It was called "Red Woods" back then. Barges would make their way up an estuary that ran to about where Interstate 280 crosses now. There they'd be loaded up with the redwood cut and processed by the sawmills in these hills.

In 1854 Doctor Robert Tripp opened a general store just off Woodside Road. "Doc" Tripp, as he was called, also served as the town's banker, its postmaster, its doctor, and even its dentist. A good pair of pliers was about all he'd need. Each day two stagecoaches would stop in front of his store on their way to settlements out by the ocean. Some of those people liked what they saw and stayed. The town prospered and that led to the hotel-saloon, and a firehouse, and eventually a schoolhouse.

Today, 5,000 people live within the town limits of Woodside, although most of the houses are well-camouflaged amid all the greenery. Some of these folks are very rich; and most of them are very committed to keeping Woodside just as it is: no sidewalks, no streetlights, lots of open space, and one of San Mateo County's best-kept secrets.

☞ Where to go and what to do:

Doc Tripp's General Store (museum), Kings Mountain and Tripp Road. Open Tuesdays and Thursdays 10:00 am to 4:00 pm, Saturday 12:00 pm to 4:00 pm. 415-851-7615.

Pioneer Saloon, 2925 Woodside Road.

FILOLI MANSION. *A 36,000-square-foot mansion on 650 acres. The house is best known as the sight of television's "Dynasty" and the Warren Beatty movie "Heaven Can Wait." The mansion was designed by Willis Polk and guilded with 200 pounds of gold. For tour information: 415-364-2880.*

MAY DAY PARADE. *Every May 7th (or thereabouts), Woodside holds an old-fashioned small-town parade. Sort of a time warp back to 1962.*

HOW TO GET THERE:

From San Francisco and the Peninsula:
Take Interstate 280 to the Woodside exit, then go west, and follow the windy road right into town.

From the East Bay:
Take the San Mateo Bridge to Interstate 280. Take 280 south (toward San Jose) to the Woodside exit, then turn right (west) and follow the road into town.

half moon bay

Deep in the fog along the California coast is a little town named after the curve of its coastline: Half Moon Bay. A Portuguese fishing village once, this is where Bay Area families come every October to search out the perfect jack-o-lantern. Half Moon Bay's damp, overcast climate is ideal for squash — and for some human beings. The fog and mist seem to accentuate the moody, brooding feel of this place.

Half Moon Bay's main street is kind of half tourist attraction, half Old West, and a store simply named Feed and Fuel seems to have captured both perfectly. Feed and Fuel sells everything from bunny rabbits to bunny chow, as well as baby chicks, turkeys, geese, and all manner of fowl. Also saddles, boots, and even ferret shampoo. (No kidding.) They've also got a rooster mascot who's clearly the cock-of-the-block. His name's Chicken Hawk.

Half Moon Bay still has a lot of farmland around it, and lots of horses due to the great trails and flat, wide-open beaches to ride. It's kind of the way America used to be: not crowded and everybody knows each other. There is something charmingly folksy about walking into the Main Street Grill and hearing the chef break into an old Western ballad as he flips eggs on the grill; they just don't allow that in the big city anymore.

Half Moon Bay seems to draw a certain kind of person. As one resident put it, "You go to the grocery store and people know you. The city is a little cold for that kind of thing." And Half Moon Bay, buried in the fog and mist, is warm.

WHERE TO GO AND WHAT TO DO:

Feed and Fuel, *331 Main Street. 415-726-5300.*

Barbara's Fish Trap. *A great little snack shack right on Half Moon Bay harbor. It's not fancy, but the prices are very reasonable and the fish is fresh. Try the fried squid.*

San Benito House, *356 Main Street. An old-fashioned country inn just packed with charm for those romantic overnights. Reserve well ahead as this place books up months in advance. There's also an excellent, but quite expensive, restaurant and bar. 415-726-3425.*

MOSS BEACH, *along Highway 1 just north of Half Moon Bay. This is also the Fitzgerald Marine Reserve where you'll find tidepools filled with tiny crabs, anemones, sea urchins, and mussels.*

HOW TO GET THERE:

From San Francisco and the Peninsula:
Interstate 280 to Highway 92 west. Highway 92 twists and turns and eventually drops down into the heart of Half Moon Bay.

From the East Bay:
Cross the San Mateo Bridge (Highway 92) and follow it through the mountains right into town.

felton

Snuggled up against the Santa Cruz Mountains, the town of Felton is half suburb, half ranchland. It's a place where people keep horses in their front yards, and their backyards are as far as the eye can see.

Coming down Graham Hill on the main road into town there is suddenly an explosion of colors, and hues, and light. Somehow, even on a damp, frost-covered morning, the sun seems to shine on little Felton; it feels like home. A number of residents say they moved away and found themselves aching for the mountain foliage and scenery. So they moved back.

But Felton's beauty and tranquility have not come without a fight. The city is encroaching. There is pressure to build new homes. Perhaps the one thing saving the town is that it doesn't have a sewer system, so there can't be much new construction. Residents say, only half in jest, that they want people to know they live in paradise and that everyone else will have to stay over the hill and just come visit.

Felton recently voted down a proposal to put parking meters along its main street. What you will see, though, are sandwich boards out in front of a burger shop that offer 10 percent off your burger if you "drive American." Some might call that small-minded isolationist; others would see it as small-town charm.

☞ WHERE TO GO AND WHAT TO DO:

Felton's main street (Highway 9) is a perfect place to stroll, particularly if you like antiques and handicrafts.

FELTON COVERED BRIDGE. *The bridge was built in 1892 and is an old wood-planked span with a shingle roof. It's at the edge of town on Covered Bridge Road.*

HENRY COWELL REDWOODS STATE PARK. *This nearby spot offers 4,000 acres of redwoods to explore.*

ROARING CAMP AND BIG TREES NARROW GAUGE RAILROAD. *A real steam engine takes you on a roller coaster ride through the Santa Cruz Mountains over to Bear Mountain (a great picnic area). The railroad station is on Graham Hill Road. 408-335-4484.*

How to get there:

From San Francisco and the Peninsula:
The fast way is Highway 101 south to Highway 17. Go west (right) over the hill to Mt. Hermon Road, turn right. At Graham Road, turn right into Felton. The scenic route would be Interstate 280 to Highway 85. Go west (right) on Highway 9, then into Felton.

From the East Bay:
Take Highway 880 south to Highway 17 west, and proceedd as above.

pacifica

For those who like a little brine in their diet, a cool mist on their face, and the smell of salt in the air, the city of Pacifica is just the place — a spot where the whitecaps come crashing in by the hour, and the fog rolls in almost every night.

Pacifica is sort of on the forgotten side of San Mateo County. It's along Highway 1 only minutes from San Francisco, but in texture and feel Pacifica is worlds away. Pacifica residents proudly proclaim that they don't have to wear suits here; that's what you do when you go to the city.

Pacifica's claim to fame is that Spanish explorer Don Gaspar Portola landed here, climbed to the top of Sweeney Ridge, and sighted San Francisco Bay. That was in 1769. These days, Pacifica is famous for its surfing (some of the most challenging — and most dangerous — waves on the continent) and for its fishing: perch, salmon, crab. You don't need a license to fish in Pacifica, just a fishing pole and a lot of time. Some folks go crabbing off the Pacifica pier. It's open 24 hours a day.

Part of Pacifica's attraction for the 38,000 people who live here is that it isn't manicured and perfect. Pacifica is still a little rough around the edges, a little wild. It still has a lot of open land, hills to climb, great bike trails, places to dive.

And, residents say, there is one other feature they like. Pacifica is not trendy; it's not a tourist attraction. In fact, most people have no idea of the wonders here. When they think about Pacifica they think of fog. And that suits the people who do live here just fine.

☞ Where to go and what to do:

Pacifica Municipal Pier, *at the foot of Santa Rosa Avenue. Open 24 hours a day for fishing. At different times of the year salmon, perch, kingfish, and crab are all pulled out of the ocean from here. No fishing license required. For information on what fish are running, call the Pacifica Pier Concession, the little bait shop right at the foot of the pier. 415-355-0690.*

We also recommend walking along the cliffs above one of the Bay Area's best-hidden beaches, Thornton State Beach. Take Highway 1 to the Manor Drive exit. Stay to the right, then turn right on Monterey Road. Drive past the McDonald's to Palmetto Avenue, then left on Westline Drive to the park entrance.

HOW TO GET THERE:

From San Francisco:

Take Highway 1 south. Exit at Francisco Boulevard, then take the next right turn and drive right to the beach.

From the Peninsula:

Interstate 280 to the Pacifica exit. Take it to Francisco Boulevard, turn right after you exit the freeway, and drive to the beach.

From the East Bay:

Take the San Mateo Bridge (Highway 92), then head north (right) on Interstate 280. Take the Pacifica exit and follow it to Francisco Boulevard. Take the first right turn off the freeway, and drive to the beach.

The scenic route:

Highway 92 from either Highway 101 or Interstate 280 drops you down into Half Moon Bay, and intersects with Highway 1. Head north on Highway 1 (right turn) for a great cliffside ride past the aptly named Devil's Slide area and then into Pacifica.

san mateo marina lagoon

ONE OF SAN MATEO COUNTY'S BEST-KEPT SECRETS IS A LITTLE SALTWATER LAGOON TUCKED AWAY IN A NONDESCRIPT RESIDENTIAL NEIGHBORHOOD JUST OFF HIGHWAY 92. UP UNTIL A FEW YEARS AGO THIS WATERWAY WAS A SHALLOW SLOUGH. THE COUNTY HAD ONLY ENOUGH MONEY TO REBUILD THE RICKETY OLD BOATHOUSE, SO IT ASKED THE STATE TO COME IN AND DREDGE THE WATERWAY AND CREATE A LAGOON. WHILE THEY WERE AT IT THEY ALSO PUT IN A BEACH. THE RESULT IS A MINIATURE RECREATIONAL AREA FOR THOSE WHO DON'T WANT TO RIDE THE WILD SURF OF HALF MOON BAY OR PACIFICA OR RISK THE UNDERTOW AT OCEAN BEACH.

You could say Marina Lagoon is "family size," just right for the kids to splash around in and for older children to "skimboard" on. A skimboard is a flat, round disk on which you slide along the water's edge. The particular advantage of this beach is its shallowness, making it very safe and allowing beleaguered parents to keep an eye on their feisty tykes while they catch some rays.

For the older and bolder there are other water sports including windsurfing, sailing, kayaking and, over the summer, sailing camp. The lagoon is small enough so that the budding sailors can never get too far away and shallow enough so they can't really get into trouble.

Many city dwellers travel hundreds of miles to go to a lake, never realizing they've got this one right in their backyard. And it's so private that on some days you may have the entire beach to yourself. San Mateo's little secret.

☞ **WHAT TO DO:**

Marina Lagoon is open dawn to dusk. The boathouse is open most days from May 1 to October 1 and rents paddleboats, sailboats, kayaks, and windsurfing equipment. The lagoon also has picnic facilities.

HOW TO GET THERE:

From San Francisco and the Peninsula:
Take Highway 101 to Highway 92, then look for the small sign reading "Fashion Mall." Follow that road and turn left at Norfolk, then follow the blue signs.

From the East Bay:
Take the San Mateo Bridge (Highway 92), then proceed as above.

3

Marin–Sonoma

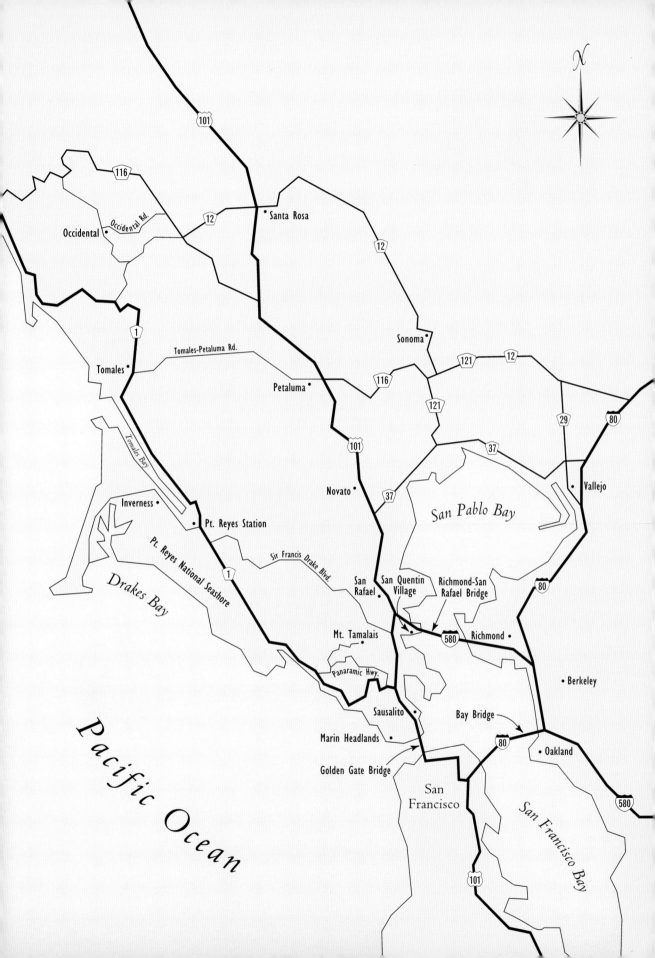

tomales

Up along the northern tip of Marin County and inland along the Shoreline Highway is Tomales. It's pretty much a blink in the road. Blink — and it's past. But stop, and you're in for a serene change of scene.

Look around at the houses, the architecture, the rolling hills, that little church. The William Tell house looks like it's 200 years old. And the National Bank looks like it could have been robbed by Jesse James. In fact, that bank is the Novato National Bank, built in Jesse James's time, 1875. Of course, Diekman's General Store across the street predates it. Diekman's has been here since the 1860s.

Some residents say they've moved away from Tomales — or run away. But they all seem to come back. Perhaps it's the picturesque charm, or the quiet life. Tomales is a good place to live if you like to relax. Everyone knows everyone else. There's so little traffic that children ride their bicycles down the town's main street — except when the tourists pour in on nice weekends. Other days, though, Tomales is like a hideaway.

Residents also say it's the best place in the whole world to go trick-or-treating on Halloween. That's because here even the adults get in costume. Some homes become haunted, and through the streets there is the eerie sound of ghouls and goblins prowling. Out here, far from the city lights, it can make for a downright frightful time.

☞ **WHERE TO GO AND WHAT TO DO:**

DIEKMAN'S GENERAL STORE, *27005 Shoreline Highway (at Dillon Beach Road).*

U.S. HOTEL, *right next door to Diekman's. An elegant, period piece in itself.*

HOG ISLAND OYSTER COMPANY, *20215 Highway 1 (about a 15-minute drive heading south from Tomales.) Not to be missed. This working oyster farm produces Pacific Oysters, as well as the French, Kumamoto (Japanese), and Eastern Oyster. It's open on weekends to look and buy. Weekdays by appointment.*

DILLON BEACH. *This beach is right at the mouth of Tomales Bay and is one of the few places you can go clamming during certain times of the year. Boat rentals also available. Take Dillon Beach Road west from Tomales to get there.*

How to get there:

From the Bay Area:

Highway 101 north to Petaluma. Go
west on Bodega Avenue, which turns into
Tomales-Petaluma Road and will take
you right into town. (Don't blink.)

san quentin village

MAGNIFICENT VIEWS. REASONABLE PRICES. AND ALMOST NO CRIME. SOUNDS LIKE SOMETHING OUT OF A REAL ESTATE BROCHURE DOESN'T IT? DID WE MENTION YOUR OWN PRIVATE BEACH? AND A CONVENIENT MARIN COUNTY LOCATION? WELCOME TO SAN QUENTIN VILLAGE, ON THE FORGOTTEN SIDE OF MARIN COUNTY. A NICE LITTLE SECRET, RESIDENTS SAY. AND ONE THEY'D LIKE TO KEEP.

This cluster of homes grew up around San Quentin State Prison in the late 18th century as a place for the warden and other employees to live. Elders remember how the town would get real quiet every Friday when the prison carried out its weekly hangings.

For the most part, this little village was mostly ignored by everyone until about 10 years ago when a batch of condos went up. The population today is a bulging 84 people — and a few dozen herons. They nest here, perhaps because it's so peaceful.

It's also affordable. Two-bedroom beachfront condos go for a fraction of what they'd cost anywhere else in this affluent and highly desirable county. Yes, the villagers do have to put up with jokes, and there *is* a big ugly prison looming in the background. But residents of San Quentin Village say they never really notice it; they say the prison is a good neighbor. And, talk about security! San Quentin Village is a very, very safe place.

☞ **WHERE TO GO AND WHAT TO DO:**

SAN QUENTIN VILLAGE BEACH. *Open during daylight hours.*

SAN QUENTIN MUSEUM. *Open 10:00 am to 4:00 pm Monday through Friday; noon to 3:00 pm Saturday; 11:00 am to 3:00 pm Sunday.*

HANDICRAFT STORE. *Just outside the prison grounds is a small shop that sells items made by the inmates. It's worth a stop, though the shop's hours are erratic.*

How to get there:

From San Francisco and the Peninsula:
Take Highway 101 to the Richmond Bridge exit, and follow that road toward the bridge. Take the San Quentin exit just before the bridge, then turn right at the first intersection, and you're there.

From the East Bay:
Interstate 80 to the Richmond Bridge. As soon as you're off the bridge, take the San Quentin exit, then follow the road into town.

petaluma

Those who grew up in Northern California probably think of Petaluma as the place with all the chickens. The town used to call itself "The Chicken Capital of the World." And it was. Every Saturday the farmers and chicken ranchers and others congregated in town to have a nice long chat. Old-timers say it would take you an hour to walk one block.

Of course that small town of the '40s has been surrounded by a new, modern, and faster-paced Petaluma. What's left of the old town is pretty much confined to a couple of blocks downtown, although plenty of the old-town attitude is still around.

Petaluma's mayor says folks who live here are people who like the "American way": family, religion, and a home. Good Americans in good old-fashioned Victorians or whitewashed clapboard-shingle homes.

Petaluma prides itself in being a little old-fashioned. You can park on the main street and stay as long as you like. The local coffee shop still offers a Blue Plate Special. There was a big controversy of late when a clothing store called Grammy Goose was forced to change its name because it sounded too much like the big potato chip maker.

You can't stop progress though. After years of turning it down, the city council finally approved the construction of a factory outlet mall in Petaluma. It's right near the old chicken ranches on the edge of town.

WHERE TO GO AND WHAT TO DO:

OLD PETALUMA. *The city's historic district is centered around Petaluma Boulevard and Washington Street. There you'll find many restored Victorians, restaurants, galleries, and antique shops. Right next to it is the turning basin, where boats swing around after their trip up the Petaluma River. The entire district is about four square blocks and, of course, the only way to really see it is on foot.*

Formal tours are available that will take you through some of the chicken ranches and produce farms. There is also a six-block Victorian home tour. Tour maps are available at 799 Baywood Drive, Suite One. For more information, call 415-769-0429.

PETALUMA FACTORY OUTLET MALL, *on Corona Road to the north of town.*

HOW TO GET THERE:

From San Francisco, the Peninsula, and the East Bay:

Cross the Golden Gate (or Richmond-San Rafael) bridges, and take Highway 101 north to Petaluma. Exit at Washington Street, then head west (left). Make another left at Petaluma Avenue, and you're in the downtown area.

occidental

OCCIDENTAL. THAT'S THE PLACE NEAR THE SONOMA COUNTY COAST WHERE FOLKS STOP FOR A BIG MEAL. ITALIAN FOOD, LOTS OF COURSES, FAMILY STYLE. THAT'S WHAT OCCIDENTAL IS FAMOUS FOR. BUT IT'S NOT WHAT THIS PLACE IS REALLY ABOUT.

Occidental and the half-dozen little towns around it are farm country, full of apple orchards and cowpies, and the folks who live here are built in that independent, western, do-it-myself style. One resident puts it this way, "Lots of people around here are doers instead of talkers."

Occidental started out as a logging town. The train used to stop here on its way to Camp Meeker, a popular resort back then. Occidental had a big Italian-American population, and a couple of good places for dinner, so that's what it became known for. Today, those old restaurants are still packing in the tourists, especially on the weekends.

But the lure for the locals is the same one that attracts so many city dwellers to small, out-of-the-way Northern California towns: you can live here in relative peace. Folks here say when you live in this part of the country you don't need tranquilizers and sleeping pills.

No stress, no crime, and, as one sweet little grandmother so quaintly put it, "the unmistakable aroma of home." Her children all live in Sacramento now, and she visits them on weekends. She says that on the way home, passing Petaluma and Bodega Bay, she'll smell the cow pastures and think, "Oh, that smells good. I'm home."

☞ **WHERE TO GO AND WHAT TO DO:**

HIGHWAY 1. *Heading out of Occidental, you through some picturesque country: thick forest land, then rolling mountains and the raging Pacific.*

BODEGA BAY. *This fishing village was the backdrop for Alfred Hitchcock's "The Birds," and they are plentiful. Herons, pelicans, and egrets feed along this shore.*

RESTAURANTS. *Occidental's restaurants offer "family style" Italian food.*

Translation: A plate of peppers, olives and salami as an appetizer; then soup, salad, and your choice of basic pasta dishes served in a red sauce. It's not fancy, but it is filling.

HOW TO GET THERE:

From the Bay Area:

Highway 101 north to Highway 12 west (left). Then take Highway 116 north (right) to Occidental Road. Make a left turn onto Occidental Road, and take it into town.

inverness

INVERNESS, ON THE BANKS OF TOMALES BAY, IS PERHAPS THE MOODIEST AND LOVELIEST OF THE STRING OF VILLAGES THAT RUN ALONG THE NORTHERN CALIFORNIA COAST. BACK IN THE LATE 1800s WEALTHY SAN FRANCISCANS BUILT THEIR SUMMER HOMES OUT HERE. THEY'D RIDE THE TRAIN TO POINT REYES STATION AND CATCH THE FERRY ACROSS THE BAY. INVERNESS WAS WHERE YOU WENT FOR A PEACEFUL SUMMER VACATION.

Today, Inverness is chock-full of country inns and pristine bed and breakfast establishments. People come for the sailing in the summer and to watch the whales in the winter. The rest of the year they come for the mood; the fog and the quiet seem to give this place a special feel.

Part of that is the light; it seems to be diffused and never glaring. You could say the atmosphere is soft, rarely harsh. Vladimir Nevl, owner of Vladimir's restaurant, calls it "complex." He should know. Vladimir himself is part Austrian, part Czech, part entrepreneur, and part showman. He stomps around his restaurant in knee-high leather riding boots and almost insists diners cap off their meals with a slice of rich European torte and a shot of Slivovitz, a clear and lethal liquor that seems to burst into flame as it travels down the gullet.

Outside, you'll cool off in the fog. Some see Inverness as a moody, brooding kind of place. Others say it's very romantic. Locals say some people move here from suburbia — and hate it. There are no movie theaters, and there's not much to do except enjoy the enchanting scenery: the bay, the parks, the seashore. Vladimir says he wants to die here. Eventually.

☞ WHERE TO GO AND WHAT TO DO:

VLADIMIR'S RESTAURANT, *Inverness Way. Features such unusual dishes as rabbit, poppyseed dumpling "Klenek," and roast duck.*

SHAKER WORKSHOP, *Inverness Way. Filled with early-American art, crafts, quilts, needlepoint, and household items.*

For a listing of some quality bed and breakfast spots, call 415-663-1420, or write the Inns of Point Reyes, P.O. Box 145, Inverness, CA 94937.

HOW TO GET THERE:

From the Bay Area:

Highway 101 to the San Anselmo/Sir Francis Drake exit. Follow Sir Francis Drake Boulevard all the way out to Point Reyes Station, where it will break off from Highway 1 and take you right into Inverness.

marin headlands

THIS AREA WAS ARMY LAND UNTIL THE EARLY '70s; NO ONE ELSE COULD EVEN GET CLOSE BECAUSE THE ARMY KEPT ITS NIKE MISSILES BURIED IN THESE HILLS. ONCE THE ARMY LEFT, FOLKS BEGAN EXPLORING THE HEADLANDS AND REALIZED HOW SPECIAL A SPOT IT WAS, ONE OF ONLY A HANDFUL OF LOCATIONS IN THE UNITED STATES WHERE YOU CAN WATCH THESE BIG BIRDS ON THEIR MIGRATORY TREK. ONE PARTICULAR PEAK THAT OFFERS A SWEEPING VIEW OF THE HILLS AND VALLEYS HAS BEEN NICKNAMED HAWK HILL, AND ON EVERY PLEASANT FALL DAY YOU'LL FIND FOLKS MAKING THE SHORT CLIMB TO THE TOP OF IT TO ENJOY THE AERIAL SHOW.

There aren't any "rides," and the animals don't ever "perform," but the Marin Headlands has a fascinating set of attractions to offer.

The Raptors. Beginning around mid-September every year thousands of America's biggest birds of prey pass through the headlands on their flight path to warmer southern climates. These magnificent birds use the Headlands' jet stream as a rest stop on the way. With or without binoculars you may catch a bald eagle, vulture, golden eagles, and hawks swooping about.

Marine Mammal Center. An unadorned slab of asphalt out on the foggy edge of the Headlands is fast becoming the Bay Area's newest attraction. The Marine Mammal Center: hospital for the creatures of the sea.

On any given day 30 to 50 seals and sea lions will be "in treatment" here — for gunshot wounds, gill-net cuts, or toxic poisoning.

The center started out in 1976 with one water hose and a couple of kiddie wading pools. Now it's got a two-million-dollar budget, a paid staff of 35, and hundreds of volunteers.

The center has found that people have a real fascination with animals that live in the ocean. They usually can't get quite as close to them as they can to land species. If you get there mid-morning you might catch these giant animals barking for their breakfast herring, or being given an antiseptic shower. (They're not crazy about that.)

Mountain Lions and Bobcats. There is one more attraction in the Headlands, but it's a little harder to see and just about impossible to photograph: mountain lions, stalking prey through the willow trees and coyote brush. At least National Park Service rangers think they're here. There are a lot of deer in these hills, and rangers say mountain lions are pretty much deer specialists.

What they do know for sure however is that these hills are populated with perhaps a dozen bobcats traipsing through the high brush. Some have radio transmitter collars on them so researchers can study their migration and feeding patterns.

☞ WHERE TO GO AND WHAT TO DO:

The Headlands are open to the public every day. Bring your binoculars, and a camera!

HAWK HILL, *at the end of Conzelman Road where it becomes one-way. Birds begin coming through around mid-August. September and October are prime bird-watching months.*

MARINE MAMMAL CENTER, *just north of Rodeo Beach. The center is open every day from 10:00 am to 4:00 pm. There is no fee, but a donation will get you a smile.*

RODEO BEACH, *at the end of Bunker Road. A lovely lagoon is attached to it as well as a sandbar island. Great beach for kids.*

HOW TO GET THERE:

From San Francisco, the East Bay, and the Peninsula:

Cross the Golden Gate Bridge. Exit at Alexander Avenue and turn left. It will take you underneath the roadway. Stay to the right and the road will curve up into the hills. This is Conzelman Road.

To get to Hawk Hill, stay on this road until it becomes one-way, then park wherever you can. To get to the Marine Mammal Center, take the first right off Conzelman, then turn left on Bunker Road and follow the signs to Rodeo Beach. At the fork in the road turn right and it will take you to the Center. To get to the bobcat area, take the first right off Conzelman, then turn right on Bunker Road and follow it into the valley. Confused? Call the Golden Gate National Recreation Area at 415-388-2595.

mount tamalpais

You've probably noticed Mt. Tamalpais poking up through the clouds some pleasant spring day. But have you ever seen what the world looks like from up there? 2,571 feet above sea level, up on the east peak of "Mt. Tam," the view is stunning. It isn't that this mountain is so tall; rather, it's the location that makes for the fantastic vista. Even without binoculars you can make out Mt. St. Helena to the north, Mt. Diablo to the southeast, and all the way to the city of Pacifica and Loma Prieta mountain due south. There is a certain feeling of reverence you get up here. The Bay Area appears to be a tender place, and you feel like you're in the middle of the sky.

As mountains go, Mt. Tam is relatively young, perhaps a couple of million years old. By contrast, the Sierra range has existed for more than 15 million years. Mt. Tamalpais is not a volcano, just a rock that's been forced up from the San Andreas Fault.

The rock has quite a history, though. Back in the 1800s the more adventuresome used to take a ferry across the Bay to Marin, and then climb aboard the Mt. Tam steam train for a steep climb to just below the summit where a parking lot is now. But the real thrill was the trip down: a white-knuckle gravity car run almost straight down, ending up at Muir Woods.

Those were the days. The train was shut down in 1935 and despite a number of attempts, it hasn't been replaced. Now you can drive to the parking lot below the summit, but you've got to hike the rest of the way up. Which has kept the peak a very serene place.

☞ WHERE TO GO AND WHAT TO DO:

THE PELICAN INN, *along Route 1 in Muir Beach. 415-383-6000. The Pub downstairs is a perfect place to rehydrate after your mountain hike. The Pub and adjoining hotel are done up to resemble England of the 1700s. Specialties include bangers, meat pies, and the like.*

STINSON BEACH, *along Route 1. Fog or sun, Stinson is lovely. Watch the birds, or stroll a gently curving three miles of sandy beach.*

RED ROCK BEACH, *along Route 1, just south of Stinson Beach. This is a great sunbathing beach, but be forewarned: the politically correct attire here is no attire. Voyeurs are discouraged.*

How to get there:

From San Francisco and the Peninsula:
Highway 101 to the Mill Valley (Highway 1) exit. Follow the signs to the Panoramic Highway, then go right and it will take you up the mountain.

From the East Bay:
Take the Richmond-San Rafael Bridge, then go south on Highway 101 to the Mill Valley (Highway 1) exit. Follow the signs to the Panoramic Highway and make a right turn. The road will lead you up the mountain.

sonoma

Like much of the wine that is produced in the Napa and Sonoma valleys, the town of Sonoma is a blend: part high-tech, gentrified, politically and environmentally correct city; part slow-paced, old-style stagecoach town. Sonoma grew up around a Spanish-style town square, or plaza. The Sonoma Mission, the last one built by Father Junipero Serra, still stands on one corner; a two-story adobe army barracks stretches along most of the north side. The barracks were built during the 1830s to house the troops of Mexican General Mariano Guadalupe Vallejo.

Today, wine shops and fancy boutiques surround those relics, including the Sonoma Cheese Company. The store carries an incredible assortment of cheeses, meats, wines, and everything else you might need for a picnic on the square. But the real fun goes on out back where the factory makes jack cheese.

If it's too late for lunch, you might head down the street to the bar at the Swiss Hotel. This place is also done in adobe and dates to the 1800s. Or, just hang out in the plaza itself, and watch the ducks and the children. The children are in the playground, the ducks in the pond. You could do a lot worse.

HOW TO GET THERE:

From the Bay Area:
Highway 101 north across the Golden Gate Bridge. Go east (right) on Highway 116, then north (left) on Highway 12 into Sonoma.

From the East Bay:
Take Interstate 80 East to Highway 29 North, then west (turn left) on Highway 12/121 to Sonoma

❋ ❋ ❋

☞ **WHERE TO GO AND WHAT TO DO:**

DEPOT PARK MUSEUM, *270 First Street East. Features an eclectic collection of paintings and artifacts from the 1800s. 707-938-9765.*

TRAIN TOWN, *20264 Broadway. Steam engines pull miniature cars through a Western town. Kids will adore. 707-938-3912.*

PLACE DES PYRENNES, *460 First Street East. A curious collection of small art, ceramics, and jewelry produced by Sonoma area artists.*

4

East Bay

piedmont avenue

Back in the 1940s and '50s, Piedmont Avenue at 41st was where you caught a Key System train for a slow, scenic journey to San Francisco and Marin. The triangle-shaped restaurant on the corner used to be a Key System station. This neighborhood centerpiece was almost taken out by the wrecker's ball a decade or so back. But tenacious community activist types saved it, and now it's just been restored and its rusted-out clock tower completely rebuilt.

Over the years many shop owners have restored their own buildings, taking them back to how they might have looked about 50 years ago, with old-fashioned awnings and interiors. Some of the shop names are from another time, too, like Morris Brandel Ability Tailor. Morris's son, Ike, took the place over from his dad some years ago, but he didn't want to take his father's name off the sign. Morris still comes in, reads the paper, goes to the bank. Ike says taking the name off would make his dad feel as though his life was finished.

Across the street, Fenton's Ice Creamery is another place that's from another time — a time when fresh cream was delivered in the morning, and two sturdy youths would spend their day in back churning it into ice cream. On warm summer nights Fenton's seems to recapture that old-time, small-town glow with customers overflowing onto the sidewalk with their rocky road sundaes and double-dipped sugar cones. And the scoops are huge.

Piedmont Avenue itself offers an appetizing assortment of the old and new. Down the block from Fenton's your senses are suddenly overwhelmed with salsa and samba emanating from the Baja Taqueria. When the weather's fine, a number of lunch places will set a couple of tables and chairs out front, all of which makes for a place people like to come to and wander around.

If you're looking for the city of Piedmont, however, don't look here; Piedmont Avenue is actually in Oakland. So is the Piedmont Theater. In fact, even the U.S. Post Office, which has a sign out front saying "Piedmont, California," is really on Oakland soil. Ask the postmaster.

How to get there:

From San Francisco and the Peninsula:

Cross the Bay Bridge and merge onto Interstate 580 east. Exit at Harrison Street, turn left on Oakland Avenue, left again on MacArthur Boulevard, then right on Piedmont Avenue. The heart of the neighborhood is around 41st.

From the East Bay:

Interstate 880 or Highway 24 to Interstate 580 east. Exit at Harrison Street, and proceed as above.

▨ ▨ ▨

☞ Where to go and what to do:

J. Hamburgers & Such *(old Key System station), 41st and Piedmont Avenue.*

Fenton's Ice Creamery, *4226 Piedmont Avenue.*

Baja Taqueria, *4070 Piedmont Avenue.*

A wonderful side trip is to the **Chapel of the Chimes,** *4499 Piedmont Avenue, at the top of Piedmont right next to the Mountain View Cemetery. Take a quiet, discreet stroll through this old-time California columbarium. It is eerie, beautiful, and full of spirits. Around Christmastime concerts for the public are held here, though they are a well-kept secret.*

clayton

L ESS THAN AN HOUR OUT OF SAN FRANCISCO, AND DIRECTLY IN THE SHADOW OF MOUNT DIABLO, IS THE TOWN OF CLAYTON — POPULATION ABOUT 8,000. YOU MIGHT SAY CLAYTON IS RIGHT ON THE FRINGE OF THE METROPOLITAN BAY AREA, WHERE THE CITY MEETS THE COUNTRY. HORSES GRAZE TWO BLOCKS FROM CITY HALL; CHICKENS CROSS MAIN STREET EACH MORNING.

In this rural setting live people who like a little space to stretch out. And that apparently includes law enforcement types. Clayton's entire police force numbers only eight, but many officers from other jurisdictions choose to live here, as well as one former San Francisco police chief and a couple of FBI agents — which may go a long way toward explaining why there's so little crime in Clayton.

The town's biggest problem is that Contra Costa County's urban sprawl keeps getting closer and closer, threatening to envelop Clayton in one of its giant housing developments. Residents say they know their wooded hideaway won't be this way forever. For the time being, though, all they've got to do is turn around and look in the other direction, toward the magnificence of Mount Diablo. The Ohlone Indians believed great power emanated from this mountain, and perhaps it does. Mount Diablo's canyons, and hillsides, and woodlands represent some of the last really wide-open space that's left in the Bay Area.

One of Mount Diablo's finest trails, the Mitchell Canyon Trail, starts from where the Clayton township ends. So, if you wanted to, you could walk out of town and keep right on going until you were 4,000 feet high. And wouldn't that be a four-star outdoor experience.

☞ WHERE TO GO AND WHAT TO DO:

THE CLAYTON CLUB, *6096 Main Street. A bar with a distinctly western twang where working folks in their steel-toe boots can hoist a cold one next to a real estate developer in his Ballys.*

MOUNT DIABLO. *We recommend Mitchell Canyon Trail, which starts on the east side of town. North Peak Trail takes you up steep slopes, but the reward is some fabulous views of the Bay Area.*

To the south there's **MORGAN TERRITORY,** *an unspoiled stretch of land where deer, rabbits, raccoon, and bobcats like to play.*

HOW TO GET THERE:

From San Francisco, the Peninsula, and the East Bay:
Highway 24 through the Caldecott Tunnel, then merge onto Interstate 680 north, and get off at Ygnacio Valley Road and go east (to the right). Turn right at Clayton Road and follow it into town.

kensington

Kensington, California, is a curiosity. Tucked between Berkeley and El Cerrito, this little unincorporated hamlet has a certain soft-spoken charm. One of Kensington's main streets, for example, is a traffic circle, a "traffic circus" residents like to call it, like London's Picadilly Circus. The Kensington Circus has been around for ages, but just a few years ago locals planted a garden in the middle, and up sprouted new businesses including a clock shop, cafe, vintage clothing store, and, naturally enough, an English-style pub.

Kensington is the kind of place you'd call quaint. It's green, and exceedingly quiet. There is no city hall in Kensington, no board of supervisors or impassioned protests, not even a city plan. A very different feel and scene from that city right next door that the people here refer to as "the People's Republic of Berkeley."

Not that the people here are isolated anarchists; they aren't. They're regular old democrats and republicans and independents who are tired of the constant pull and tug of sandbox politics.

Consequently, there aren't too many demonstrations in Kensington, but there are a lot of Tudors. The Old English flavor runs heavy here. In fact, you might say that's the theme of the town. It's very neighborhoody, and much more interesting to walk through than drive. Especially the circus.

☞ **Where to go and what to do:**

The Vintage Clothing Store, *396 Colusa Avenue. Perhaps the best collection of men's used, high-fashion clothing in the Bay Area. Hats, tuxedos, spats. Not to be missed.*

Colusa Market, *406 Colusa Avenue. A very pleasant, old-fashioned grocery store with that lovely, sweet, cool aroma that only old markets seem to have.*

HOW TO GET THERE:

From San Francisco and the Peninsula:
Take the Bay Bridge, then stay to the left and get onto Interstate 80 east. Take the Gilman Street exit and go east (right). Turn left on San Pablo Avenue, then turn right on Solano Avenue and follow it to the top. Make a left onto Colusa Avenue and go about two miles to the circle.

From the East Bay:
Interstate 80 east, exit at Gilman Street and go east (right). Proceed as above.

canyon

HIDDEN IN A LUSH VALLEY BETWEEN THE TOWN OF MORAGA AND THE OAKLAND HILLS IS CANYON — POPULATION 250, OR SO THE POSTMASTER CLAIMS. DRIVING THROUGH CANYON YOU DON'T SEE ANY TOWN. NO HOMES, NO STORES, ONLY AN OCCASIONAL CAR.

Canyon was a logging town once. Then in the turbulent 1960s it was known for its drug activity — the kind of place you could go if you needed to "fade away" from the law. Today, Canyon is hardly known at all, and Canyonites like it that way. Peaceful, and a far cry from what's just over the hill in the city.

Canyon actually has a couple of hundred homes hidden in its acres of tall redwoods and ranging chaparral. Some you can only get to by hiking up a more-or-less unmarked path. These people aren't hillbillies; they have TVs and computers and all the other conveniences of modern life. But they also have the kind of solitude that is almost nonexistent in the Bay Area.

One long-time Canyonite said living here is kind of like living in a poem or a dream. Visitors can come and enjoy the poem if they'd like, but they can't live it. There's rarely any land for sale in Canyon, and you wouldn't be allowed to build a home here even if there was. What land there is mostly gets passed along from family to family or friend to friend. That's just the way it is — in Canyon.

☞ WHERE TO GO AND WHAT TO DO:

About the only thing you can do in Canyon is go for a beautiful Sunday drive or walk around and stop for a picnic.

Good hiking and picnic facilities are also available nearby at **SAN LEANDRO RESERVOIR** *near Pinehurst and Canyon Road. There is a small permit fee.*

HOW TO GET THERE:

From San Francisco and the Peninsula:
Cross the Bay Bridge and get onto
Interstate 580 east, then get in the right
lane and take Highway 24 toward
Berkeley. Stay on Highway 24 through
the Caldecott Tunnel, then take the
Orinda exit. Go south (right) on Moraga
Way, then right on Canyon Road, and
right again on Pinehurst.

From the East Bay:
Highway 24 through the Caldecott
Tunnel and proceed as above.

ardenwood

Look at a Bay Area map. Ardenwood Regional Preserve isn't on it. Ardenwood is an out-of-the-way spot of land just off the Bay in Newark that no one lives on and few have visited. Not human beings anyway. Ardenwood is very popular with one of the earth's other species — the bright orange Monarch butterfly.

Each November an estimated 10 to 12 thousand Monarch butterflies stop at Ardenwood for their winter vacation. They like the mild climate, the peaceful and safe setting, and the trees of Ardenwood, especially the eucalyptus. It blooms in winter and provides a nectar worth traveling for.

So many of the fragile, exquisite Monarchs come to Ardenwood that you can actually hear their tender wings fluttering. The sound is sometimes called susurrus. Park workers say they see visitors standing very still and staring up at the trees. They look and listen, and suddenly smiles break out on their faces. They've heard the susurrus.

The Monarch spends its winters mostly hanging around in the trees. The slender insect's wings won't work unless the temperature is at least 50 degrees. Then in February and March the sun begins to beam through the trees and warm the ground. The Monarch grows active and restless and begins moving around looking for food. And looking for love. The female Monarch, "Madame Butterfly" if you will, will mate with as many males as she can in order to maximize egg production.

The 200-acre parcel of land that makes up Ardenwood is, in fact, a working farm and ranch right in the middle of six million people and right off the bustling Nimitz Freeway. The East Bay Regional Park District bought the land in 1981 to save its dark, loamy soil, a huge windbreaking forest of eucalyptus trees and a beautiful 19th-century mansion from developers who wanted to scour everything to the bedrock and add on to suburbia. No one knew about the Monarch wintering here; it was a pleasant accident.

In 1985 the Park District opened Ardenwood to the public, and with it a window right back into the Bay Area's last century when high-tech was a railroad track being laid across the land and mass transit was a hayride.

And speaking of hayrides, you can still take one at Ardenwood, or walk through the 19th-century mansion, or watch the smithy hammer horseshoes in the barn. Strolling the grounds you'll also notice a burial site of the Ohlone Indians, one of the first settlers in this part of the world. The site is protected in its natural state, but there is a replica of an Ohlone village you can walk through.

Ardenwood is open from the first weekend in April through November. The butterflies arrive in November and stay through March, but you must make an appointment to visit them. Call by the second week of October before the spots fill up. Admission to Ardenwood is $6 for adults, $3.50 for children 4 to 17 and free for the little ones. There are wonderful grounds for picnics and open spaces for kids to romp. Two big "No's": no dogs and no barbecues.

HOW TO GET THERE:

From San Francisco and the Peninsula:

Take the Bayshore Freeway (Highway 101) south and merge onto Highway 92 east (toward Hayward). A few miles after you cross the bridge, merge onto Interstate 880 south. Get off at the Ardenwood Boulevard exit, then turn right and follow the signs.

From the East Bay:

Take Interstate 880 south to the Ardenwood Boulevard exit, then turn right and follow the signs.

lafayette

It's quiet, green, and the living is easy. Lafayette — named for the French general, even if he never went near the place. The town of Lafayette was born in the very late 1800s, more or less as a rest stop along the trail between San Francisco and the Contra Costa County seat in Martinez.

The Wayside Thrift Store along Mt. Diablo Boulevard used to be a hotel and tavern. The pizza place next door was a saloon. (Get the idea of what was important here?) The Park Theatre sits on what used to be the old community swimming hole. The swimming hole is long gone. It was paved over nearly a half-century ago. But the Lafayette of today still has a few popular spots.

One of them is the town's oldest coffee shop, The Squirrels. This place has developed quite a reputation among anglophiles for its bangers, an English pork sausage with what we can only call an "unusual" taste. A waitress at Squirrels says they're not like regular sausages; people either love 'em or hate 'em.

Homemade scones are perhaps a safer bet for the uninitiated. An English couple used to own Squirrels and, as the story goes, they thought it good luck to name their new business after an animal, even if a squirrel is technically a rodent.

And as long as we're telling stories, the one about how this town got its name is pretty good. It had no name, and the postmaster said it needed one. Residents settled on Centerville, but there was already one of those not far away. The founder of the town, Elum Brown, refused to let them call it Brownsville. Finally, someone said how about Lafayette, and everyone quickly went along. Eventually the town put up a statue of the Marquis de Lafayette. His connection to America is that he served in the Continental Army in the American Revolution.

They might just as well have called this place Evergreen, however, since its main attraction is its low-density, high-foilage living.

☞ WHERE TO GO AND WHAT TO DO:

Mt. Diablo Boulevard and Moraga Road is a good place to start from. This is where the saloon and hotel used to be.

LAFAYETTE RESERVOIR, west of town, just off Mt. Diablo Boulevard. Open year-round for boating and fishing. No swimming.

THE ROUNDUP, 3553 Mt. Diablo Boulevard. No trip to Lafayette is complete without a stop at The Roundup. It's one of the last old-time, rowdy, genuinely fun bars around, and a real funky contrast to the general tone of the town.

HOW TO GET THERE:

From San Francisco and the Peninsula:
Cross the Bay Bridge and merge onto Interstate 580. Get into the right lane, and take the Highway 24 (Berkeley) exit. Stay on Highway 24 through the Caldecott Tunnel. Exit at Mt. Diablo Boulevard and take that road all the way into town. Park near Moraga Road.

From the East Bay:
Take Highway 24 through the Caldecott Tunnel. Exit at Mt. Diablo Boulevard and proceed as above.

alameda

THERE IS NO FREEWAY ROUTE TO THE CITY OF ALAMEDA. TO GET THERE YOU HAVE TO GO THROUGH A TUBE, (THE POSEY TUBE) OR OVER A DRAWBRIDGE. IN OUR DOUBLE-STEP, COMMUTER-CLOGGED SOCIETY, ALAMEDA IS AN ISLAND; LITERALLY AND FIGURATIVELY. TWELVE-AND-A-HALF SQUARE MILES, 12,000 TREES, 75,000 PEOPLE. RESIDENTS SAY THEY'RE NO DIFFERENT FROM MOST CALIFORNIANS; IT'S JUST THAT THEY'RE OUT OF THE HEAVY FLOW OF LIFE — EXCEPT SOME-TIMES WHEN THEY GET STUCK IN THE TUBE.

Alameda is a place that doesn't seem to have been spoiled by change or too many people. It's a small enough city that people don't feel they've lost touch. If you're having breakfast at Ole's Waffle Shop on Park Street, and you find you forgot your wallet, that's okay. Pay next time you come in.

If Alameda is really known for anything it's probably the elegant Queen Annes, ornate Victorians, and California bungalow homes built from the mid 1800s to the 1920s. Alamedans pride themselves on restoring these painted ladies to their youthful luster.

And then, there's the feeling of safety here. Alameda has one of the lowest crime rates of any East Bay city. Residents joke that if anything bad were to happen on the "mainland," all they'd have to do is pull up the bridges, and block the tube. We might add that then they could just motorize the island, and float away.

☞ WHERE TO GO AND WHAT TO DO:

OLE'S WAFFLE SHOP, *1507 Park Street. Quintessential American diner.*

ROBERT CROWN BEACH, *along Shore Line Drive at the very end of Park Street. A couple of miles of white, sandy beach, even though it keeps washing away and the East Bay Regional Park District has to keep bringing more in.*

CRAB COVE, *at the north end of Crown Beach, is an ideal kids' beach. Shallow water, tiny waves, protected cove.*

THE GOLD COAST NEIGHBORHOOD. *This section of town is worth cruising through for its lovely mansions, especially along the waterfront. Take San Antonio Avenue and turn onto either Webster Street, Hawthorne Street, or Bay. Around Christmastime, Thompson Avenue residents go overboard decorating their houses, to the point that this street has been nicknamed "Christmas Tree Lane."*

HOW TO GET THERE:

From San Francisco and the Peninsula:
Cross the Bay Bridge and get onto Interstate 980 south, which will lead you to Interstate 880 south. Exit at Park Street, then follow the signs to the Park Street Bridge. Cross the drawbridge and you'll be on Park Street. Stop and explore whatever looks interesting.

From the East Bay:
Interstate 880 to the Park Street exit, then follow the signs to the Park Street Bridge. Crossing the old drawbridge will put you onto Park Street and into one of the commercial strips.

point richmond

THERE IS RICHMOND, AND THEN THERE IS POINT RICHMOND, A LITTLE BURG BUILT INTO THE HILLS OVERLOOKING SAN FRANCISCO BAY. FOLKS UP HERE BOAST OF HAVING THE BEST VIEWS IN THE BAY AREA: THREE BRIDGES (GOLDEN GATE, BAY BRIDGE, AND RICHMOND – SAN RAFAEL BRIDGE), THE BAY, AND ANGEL ISLAND. AND NONE OF THE TROUBLE AND THE COLDNESS YOU FIND IN THE BIG CITY.

Point Richmond is really old Richmond. Many of the homes on the hills facing the water were built at the turn of the century. This area was practically the entire town until World War II. Industrialist Henry Kaiser decided to build his Liberty Ships here, and Richmond's population boomed.

Today, Point Richmond is a tiny green jewel, surrounded by refineries and freeways and a lot of urban blight. Many people who live in Point Richmond say they stumbled upon it by accident one day. It's out of the way, not "on the map." They found it, and they stayed.

In fact, Point Richmond has a few treasures that aren't "on the map." One is a secluded, sandy bayside beach, Keller Beach. It's part of the 295-acre Miller-Knox Regional Shoreline, which also offers some terrific trails for hiking and biking and a 360-degree view from the top of the ridge.

And then there is what may be the most unusual bed and breakfast inn you'll find anywhere in the Bay Area. It's an inn that's on an offshore island, next to a lighthouse. The lighthouse beacon doesn't shine anymore, but the two-story inn is thriving. Guests are taken to this private little hideaway by motorboat. Talk about your romantic getaway. Who would've thought you'd find one right here?

☞ WHERE TO GO AND WHAT TO DO:

HIDDEN CITY CAFE, *109 Park Place. One chamber of commerce type says this place has "gourmet food at pedestrian prices."*

THE HOTEL MAC, *at 50 Washington Avenue, and* **THE BALTIC,** *located at 135 Park Place, are both worth checking out — and dining in.*

MILLER-KNOX REGIONAL SHORELINE. *To get there you've got to go through the tunnel that leads out to the Bay, then take a right once out on the point, and you'll see the beach.*

EAST BROTHER LIGHT STATION (LIGHTHOUSE INN). *Call 415-233-2385 for reservations. Book early as they're always full up. This is a perfect romantic night away. Dinner is a six-course feast and is included in the price.*

HOW TO GET THERE:

From the East Bay:

Take Interstate 80 north, then Interstate 580 into Richmond, exiting at Cutting Boulevard. Continue to Garrard Boulevard and turn left. This will take you right into the old section.

From San Francisco and the Peninsula:

Cross the Bay Bridge and take Interstate 80 north (toward Berkeley), then get onto Interstate 580 into Richmond, and proceed as above.

❈ ❈ ❈

niles

Niles, California. Never heard of it? Lots of people haven't. At one time though, Niles was California's "Hollywood," Charlie Chaplin's home, and a fairly major stop on the Transcontinental Railroad. That was back in 1869. An executive at Union Pacific Railroad named Judge Niles persuaded his company to build a station in this little East Bay town. The townsfolk were so grateful they named the town after him.

In 1913 Charlie Chaplin came here to make moving pictures at S & A Studios, turning the then sleepy suburb into a fast-moving and fast-talking place, though the movies were still silent. Along with Chaplin's pictures cowboy westerns were shot here, and the "Continuing Adventures of Bronco Billy Anderson."

Old-timers say some of those adventures continued into the weekend. As Louis Digiulio puts it, "We used to raise the devil here on Saturday nights, and they'd kind of tear the houses up around here when they had a big time. A lot of them were drunks you know."

S & A suddenly left town in 1916 amid rumors of financial problems. The town's name is still written in huge letters in the lovely hills behind the railroad tracks, just as in Hollywood. In 1956 Niles and the other hamlets around here incorporated to prevent San Jose and Hayward from annexing them. So the town of Niles became part of the town of Fremont — officially anyway. Unofficially, it's still Niles.

Actually, Niles remains part city, part farm. One side is bordered by lush, green Niles Canyon where cows still graze. The other side of the street looks like an Old West town.

Huge elm trees and finely crafted brick buildings line Niles Boulevard. Many of the buildings are filled with antique shops. The rest seem to be predominantly saloons.

The Transcontinental Railroad is gone but Amtrak's Capitol Express is coming through, from San Jose to Sacramento, three times a day. Right through Niles. Just like the old days.

☞ WHERE TO GO AND WHAT TO DO:

NILES CANYON RAILROAD MUSEUM. *Offers round-trips between Niles and Sunol through scenic Niles Canyon on the first and third Sundays of each month. Steam and diesel locomotives pull classic old railcars along the route. They run between 10:00 am and 4:00 pm, tickets are $5.00 for adults, $2.00 for children. The round-trip takes about 45 minutes. For more information, call 510-362-9063.*

We also recommend a stroll one block west of Niles Boulevard to get a feel for the old-time, small-town flavor many families have discovered in Niles. There's a lot of Old California left in this town, from the Mission Revival-style library to the ancient honeysuckle and trumpet vines climbing over sun-bleached fences.

HOW TO GET THERE:

From San Francisco and the Peninsula:
Take the San Mateo Bridge, then get onto Interstate 880 south. Take the Alvarado/Niles Road exit and go east for several miles. It will turn into Niles Canyon Road and narrow. As you get very close to the hills, you'll enter town.

From the East Bay:
Interstate 880 south to the Alvarado-Niles Road exit. Proceed as above.

jingletown

JINGLETOWN IS SURROUNDED BY FACTORIES AND FREEWAYS, TRAIN TRACKS AND BART. IT'S ALMOST ISOLATED, WHICH MAY BE THE MAIN REASON IT HAS MANAGED TO HOLD ONTO THAT CLOSE-KNIT FEEL THAT YOU DON'T FIND MUCH IN A BIG CITY LIKE OAKLAND ANYMORE. FROM 23RD AVENUE TO 29TH, BETWEEN THE NIMITZ FREEWAY AND THE BART TRACKS, THERE IS NO CRIME TO SPEAK OF. THERE ARE NO DRUGS BEING SOLD ON THE STREET CORNERS. THIS IS JINGLETOWN. PEOPLE DON'T DO THAT HERE.

Back in the 1930s and '40s, Jingletown was mostly Portuguese. The men worked in the factories, a cotton mill and the Del Monte Cannery. The neighborhood got its name because on the first and fifteenth of the month everyone would get paid in cash: silver dollars, Walking Liberty half dollars, and smaller change. All those coins would jingle around as they walked home.

The old Portuguese families have moved on, and Mexican-Americans have moved in. They have brought their love of big families, bountiful vegetable gardens, and flowers with them. Jingletown is overgrown with produce, wild roses, and bougainvillea, a reminder that East Oakland was once famous for its dark, loamy soil that could grow almost anything year-round.

There is a certain neighborhood pride that has been retained over generations here. The weather-beaten homes are scrubbed clean and in good repair. The sidewalks are tidy, and dozens of children ride their bikes safely in the uncluttered streets. Alicia Hernandez owns the neighborhood grocery store. She says folks are proud of Jingletown, and they raise their children to be proud of it, too. They feel like they're preserving a bit of Oakland's history. You might call it a living museum.

☞ **WHERE TO GO AND WHAT TO DO:**

JINGLETOWN GROCERY. *Sells Nestle's Quick, tacos, and candles for San Antonio de Padua. The church is housed in a turn-of-the-century clapboard building. Mass is still held in English and Spanish.*

How to get there:

From San Francisco and the Peninsula:
Take the Bay Bridge, then Interstate 580 east, to Interstate 980, which leads you right onto Interstate 880 south. Exit at 29th Avenue. Go east to 11th Street and turn right. Turn right again on 26th Avenue and follow it to East 9th Street where you must make a left. You are there.

From the East Bay:
Interstate 880 south to 29th Avenue exit. Go east to 11th Street and turn right, then proceed as above.

tilden park

It takes a little getting to but Tilden Park, deep in the Berkeley hills, is truly a Bay Area jewel. On its grounds you'll find an honest-to-goodness National Landmark and an authentic, if slightly downsized, railroad: The Redwood Valley Railroad.

Around 11:00 in the morning on the days that she's running, old Engine #4 will build up a head of steam, throw a billow of smoke, and head for the barn. There she'll hook up her cars and head out for the first run of the day along the railroad's mile-and-a-quarter track.

Old #4 isn't exactly full-size, but it isn't a model either. It's five-twelfths scale, about 40 percent of full size. But aside from its diminutive stature, it is the real thing: a working steam engine, smelling of valve oil, and making a racket on the tracks. These days many of the mini-railroads use gas-driven engines with tape recorders to recreate the sound. But you can't recreate the real thing. The engineers who lovingly attend to these beasts say a steam engine is probably the closest man has ever come to creating a living, breathing creature complete with idiosyncrasies; if they don't like how you care for them, they'll let you know.

The 10 minute ride through Tilden Park is authentic as well, taking you far into the woods, through a sooty tunnel, and back over a trestle overpass. For grown-ups it's nostalgia guaranteed. Kids think it's just plain cool.

Down the park's main road, you'll find another bit of magic: the Tilden Park Merry-Go-Round. This 82-year-old carousel is one of only a few "menagerie-type" merry-go-rounds still in existence. Besides horses, it has frogs, dogs, storks, goats, and a hippo-campus (sort of like a sea dragon), all hand-carved by the legendary Hirshall-Spillman Company, and all now being hand-restored by Peter and Terry Holleman.

The Hollemans took over this little piece of history a couple of years back and immediately set to cleaning, painting, and repairing the thousands of parts that had worn or tarnished with time — and to caring for the animals. The stork needed a new foot; Prancer had cracked ears. These things are important, especially if you're five. The Hollemans say they love to watch the children eyeing the animals as the carousel goes round, picking out the one that will be their special mount for the next ride.

As the carousel turns they just laugh and giggle, the kind of feeling of exhilaration you get when you stick your head out the window with the car going fast and the wind in your face. A little magic, and a lot of smiles. For a dollar a ride.

☞ WHERE TO GO AND WHAT TO DO:

REDWOOD VALLEY RAILROAD. *During the summer months the railroad operates every day between noon and 5:00 pm. The rest of the year it's open weekends only, from 11:00 am to 6:00 pm. $1.50 per ride.*

Model railroad (lower level). Trains are run here most Sundays from noon to 3:30 pm.

TILDEN PARK MERRY-GO-ROUND; *Open every weekend from 10:00 am to 5:00 pm. Summer hours vary. $1.00 per ride. Call East Bay Regional Parks at 510-562-7275 for a recorded message on operating hours.*

LAKE ANZA, *also in Tilden Park, is a favorite summer swimming hole for Berkeley residents. $2.00 for adults, $1.00 for kids. Lifeguards on weekends.*

HOW TO GET THERE:

From San Francisco, the Peninsula, and the East Bay:

Cross the Bay Bridge, then get onto Interstate 580. Get into the extreme right lane and take the Highway 24 ramp (toward Berkeley). Stay on Highway 24 through the Caldecott Tunnel. Right after the tunnel exit at Fish Ranch Road. It will loop back around and head you up the hill. Turn right at Grizzly Peak Boulevard (the first big intersection) and follow the road around the mountain for about a mile. The Steam Train is on your right. The Merry-Go-Round is another couple of miles down that same road, as is Lake Anza.

❊ ❊ ❊

oakdale *(The Hershey Factory)*

THERE'S NO BIG NEON SIGN POINTING THE WAY. IN FACT, THERE IS HARDLY ANY INDICATION AT ALL OF WHAT GOES ON INSIDE THE HUGE SINGLE-STORY, CINDER BLOCK BUILDING IN OAKDALE, CALIFORNIA. WELL, THERE *IS* ONE HINT. THE STREET LAMPS OUTSIDE ARE IN THE SHAPE OF HERSHEY KISSES. THIS IS THE PLACE WHERE CHOCOLATE IS MADE: THE HERSHEY CHOCOLATE FACTORY.

The first thing that hits you once inside the factory is the noise. Then comes the overwhelming smell of chocolate. The noise is from the Hershey Kiss line; little kisses stream out of a "claketa-claketa" machine invented by old Milton Hershey himself. The chocolate smell is even more powerful in the chocolate chip moulding room. A machine that looks and sounds like a big printing press stamps out row upon row of perfect chips.

But the gooey heart of the factory is where you develop an insatiable craving for chocolate. Here it oozes out in thick streams into huge pools called conches. Then the chocolate is gently massaged to bring out the flavor. This place is like a dream for children. Some say they want to go swimming in the pools. Many an adult has probably thought the same thing. Kisses, Reese's Peanut Butter Cups, Hershey Bars, Mr. Goodbars, chocolate syrup — all made right here.

Employees say they work around it every day, but they never get sick of it. In fact, all over the building in the employees' offices there are buckets of chocolate — the stuff that's cracked or miswrapped — for the workers to snack on. Now that's what you call a sweet job.

☞ WHERE TO GO AND WHAT TO DO:

THE HERSHEY FACTORY: *Free tours are given Monday through Friday 8:30 am to 3:00 pm. The tours run about every half hour. No tours on weekends or holidays. Tours begin at the Hershey Visitors Center at 120 South Sierra Street. A shuttle takes you to the factory from there. For more information, call 209-848-8126.*

From San Francisco, the Peninsula, and the East Bay:

Take Interstate 580 east to Interstate 205, to Highway 120 east. Go through Sonora and into Oakdale, then go one block past the street signal to G Street, and turn left.

*Hershey's, Hershey's Kisses, Reese's and Mr. Goodbar are trademarks used with permission of Hershey Foods Corporation.

5

Beyond the Bay

crockett

Along the banks of the Carquinez Strait and in the shadow of the Bay Area's oldest bridge sits the rough-hewn town of Crockett — population, about 4,000. You've probably driven by Crockett coming back from the Sierra. It's the place with the old C & H sign. C & H refines sugar here; in fact, C & H used to just about own this town. Locals called it "Sugar City." The C and H stand for California, where the sugar is processed, and Hawaii, where it's grown.

Crockett isn't what you'd call a pretty town. The Carquinez Bridge, looking like a giant erector set, looms over one side of the place. And the massive brick sugar plant dominates the waterfront. But then Crockett isn't selling "pretty." It isn't trying to become a tourist attraction. There aren't any cutesy shopping malls or restored old sections.

Of course, that lack of trying in itself has made Crockett attractive. The older guys who hang around the gas station say nearly everybody who comes in to fill up says, "Gee, what a great town, what a find. It's hard to find a little community like this."

What Crockett offers is quiet. You can walk around the streets without meeting anyone for blocks. It's a slow-paced, older-style river town: two gas stations, one hardware store, a dozen saloons, and an attitude. Folks here say they couldn't live in a big city; they couldn't stand it. Crockett does have a somewhat older population, but young people have been moving here of late attracted by low crime, low housing prices, and low stress.

And then there's the fishing. Salmon, rock cod, and bass run thick up here at different times of the year, and a half-dozen charter boat companies would love to take you out and make sure you catch your limit. Local fishermen don't bother with the charters of course. They've got their special coves and inlets and rocks. As far as most of them are concerned, they've got everything they need right here. And everything they don't need passes right by on the freeway overhead.

☞ WHERE TO GO AND WHAT TO DO:

C & H SUGAR REFINERY. *No tours, but it's still interesting to walk around this old brick complex.*

CARQUINEZ STRAIT REGIONAL SHORELINE. *This is a brand-new stretch of open space that runs along the bluffs of the Sacramento River.*

Fishing: **CROCKETT SPORT FISHING,** *Port Street. 510-787-1047.* **DELTA FISH FINDERS,** *169 West Brannan Island Road, Isleton. 916-777-6411.*

HOW TO GET THERE:

From the Bay Area:

Take Interstate 80 east all the way to just before the Carquinez Bridge, and take the Crockett exit. Pomona Drive is the main street through town, but we recommend you zig-zag back and forth getting as close to the water as you can. You can also keep going east on Pomona out of town until it turns into Carquinez Scenic Drive, and follow this windy road to the new shoreline park.

▦ ▦ ▦

rio vista

I F THE DELTA TOWN OF RIO VISTA IS FAMOUS FOR ANYTHING, IT'S PROBABLY HUMPHREY, THE HUMPBACK WHALE. IN OCTOBER OF 1985 HE SWAM INTO SAN FRANCISCO BAY AND JUST KEPT RIGHT ON GOING, PAST THE CARQUINEZ STRAIT AND UP INTO THE NARROWING DELTA. THEN HE SWAM UNDER THE BRIDGE LEADING TO RIO VISTA, AND COULDN'T GET BACK THROUGH TO THE OTHER SIDE. THE WHALE'S STRANGE ODYSSEY BROUGHT TENS OF THOUSANDS OF TOURISTS TO THE REGION AS WELL AS TELEVISION NEWS CREWS FROM ALL OVER THE PLANET, TURNING RIO VISTA INTO A MEDIA CIRCUS FOR A COUPLE OF WEEKS. UNTIL HUMPHREY GOT TIRED OF HIS TREK AND TURNED BACK. THEN, RIO VISTA WENT BACK TO BEING WHAT IT WAS BEFORE — A SLOW DELTA TOWN.

Walking through Rio Vista feels a little like walking through the set of the 1960s television series "Mayberry R.F.D." Kids lazily walk to the swimming hole (actually the community pool) every day during summer and nobody's too worried about them walking around town alone. For the most part, Rio Vistans seem to have dedicated their community to cowboys, fish, and the American flag. Along Main Street there are a whole lot of American flags, the most colorful display belonging to Papa Joe's Vista Mini Mall featuring Papa Joe's Famous Foot Longs (those are hot dogs) and penny candy. 'Course penny candy starts at a nickel these days.

The mini-mall is also where the kids hang out at night under a larger-than-life cardboard picture of a moody Elvis Presley, and, naturally, the biggest American flag you'll ever see. Another reason they're here is that there isn't much else to do. Rio Vista doesn't have a movie theatre or a bowling alley.

Residents say they like to get together and play cards, or discuss politics and gossip. They know it's kind of boring, but it's okay. Papa Joe, by the way, says he isn't ever bored. He's in his sixties. Ask him what he does at night and Papa Joe will get a pixieish gleam in his eye and tell you he "chases girls." Which certainly qualifies as another great American pastime.

 Where to go and what to do:

Papa Joe's Vista Mini Mall, *231 Main Street.*

Foster's Big Horn Bar, *143 Main Street. Hundreds of trophies, from deer antlers to elephant tusks. Must be seen to be believed.*

Brannan Island State Recreation Area, *Route 160, a few miles south of town. Good beach, great fishing, and a mess of sloughs and waterways.*

How to get there:

From the Bay Area:

Bay Bridge to Interstate 580, then Highway 24 toward Walnut Creek. Take Interstate 680 north to Highway 4; then east on Highway 4 all the way past Antioch. Next take Highway 160 north (over the bridge) to Highway 12. Go left over another bridge and into town.

pinole

Ever seen one of those elaborate model train sets with tracks swaying with the curves of the hills, running over iron bridges and under wooden ones, and past those cute little turn-of-the-century buildings accurate to the smallest detail? That's about what Pinole looks like — old Pinole at least.

Located 25 miles northeast of San Francisco, the city of Pinole grew up along its railroad tracks. In the late 1800s Pinole Landing, as it was known then, was a major port on San Pablo Bay. Tan bark, which was grown here, was shipped to Monterey to be used in tanning hides. And bombs and ammunition were shipped from the Hercules Powder Works just up the road. It's forgotten now, except by the grandchildren of some men who lost their lives in the big explosions there.

Not that much has really changed in Pinole, at least on the outside. The ornate, pillared Bank of Pinole, for example, still has its impressive facade, even though there's no bank inside anymore. The historic Fernandez Mansion still stands as well. Bernardo Fernandez, a founding father of Pinole, built it near the water back in 1894. The Mariati family bought it in the 1970s with the idea of tearing it down to build apartments. But in the end, they just couldn't bring themselves to do it. So they fixed the place up instead. Kind of tells the story of Pinole.

One city councilwoman put it another way. "You don't know where you're going until you know where you've been. And that's part of your past; that's your roots. That's what this community is founded on."

☞ WHERE TO GO AND WHAT TO DO:

POINT PINOLE REGIONAL SHORELINE, *off Interstate 80. Take Atlas Road in Richmond. The park is along San Pablo Bay: 2,000 acres of rolling lands, and salt marshes that are great for kids to explore. The beaches are full of driftwood. A fishing pier juts well out into the Bay and anglers pull in salmon, sturgeon, bass, and steelhead.*

Alongside Pinole's Fernandez Park is a creek full of frogs and maybe even a few fish. There's also a paved path running all the way to the Bay. The path also takes you to the San Pablo Bay Regional Park, a small bayside swath of green that's well away from the crowds and cars.

HOW TO GET THERE:

From the Bay Area:

Take Interstate 80 east. Exit at Appian Way, then head west (left), back under the freeway, and follow the road to San Pablo Avenue where you'll turn right. Go to the corner of Tennent Avenue and you're downtown.

❖ ❖ ❖

rodeo

Rodeo, just off Highway 80 about 20 miles north of Oakland, used to be ranch-land. They held roundups here and once a year, a really big rodeo; hence the name of the town. And then there was the fishing. This used to be a world-class fishing resort, with anglers coming from all over the country when the bass were running. They had a bass derby every year.

Some of those visitors decided to stay and built homes here, ranch-style, wood-frame homes. They planted willows and oaks out front. And peach and plum and apple trees out back. Now, the half-century-old willows provide grateful shade from the summer sun. And the peaches? Well, let's just say come August there's a whole lot of pie around.

Now this wartime boom town is debating sprucing up its neglected waterfront to bring the fishermen and the tourists back. But a lot of citizens like Rodeo the way it is: unassuming, unhurried, and a surviving piece of small-time America.

☞ **WHERE TO GO AND WHAT TO DO:**

Pacific Avenue is the main street through town, ending at a truly old industrial marina. There are a couple of interesting, if funky, waterside eateries here including **THE SILVER DOLLAR II.** *It's across the bridge on the right-hand side.*

For fishing, check in at the **RODEO SPORT AND TAXIDERMY SHOP** *at 360 Parker Avenue. If you get lucky and catch a massive sturgeon, you can have it mounted here as well.*

HOW TO GET THERE:

From the Bay Area:

Take Interstate 80 east; exit onto Highway 4 west (left) which takes you back under the freeway. Turn right on San Pablo Avenue, and travel north about a mile into Rodeo. Make a left on Pacific Avenue.

benicia

THIRTY-SEVEN MILES NORTHEAST OF SAN FRANCISCO, AND RIGHT ON THE CARQUINEZ STRAIT, SITS THE CITY OF BENICIA. THERE IS A CERTAIN "SOUTHERN FEEL" TO MANY TOWNS ALONG THE SACRAMENTO DELTA, AND NOWHERE IS IT MORE PRONOUNCED THAN HERE. SECOND-FLOOR BALCONIES WITH A SLIGHT SAG JUT OUT OVER TALL AND ORNATE ENTRYWAYS; LUSH GREEN VINES CLIMB THE SIDES OF THE OLDER, CLAPBOARD-SHINGLE HOMES; AND THE WHOLE TOWN HAS THAT SLOWER, ALMOST LAZY PACE THAT YOU NEVER FEEL IN THE BIG CITIES JUST A HALF-HOUR AWAY. UP HERE THE FOLKS CALL THOSE CITY DWELLERS "THE PEOPLE ACROSS THE POND," REFERRING TO THE CARQUINEZ STRAIT.

Back in the 1840s, this part of Northern California was controlled by a general, Mariano Vallejo. A man named Robert Sample persuaded General Vallejo that a town should be founded here and shrewdly suggested it be named for the general's wife, Francisca Benicia Vallejo. Sample meant for the town to be called "Francisca." Well, officials of a nearby city, then known as Yerba Buena, objected and immediately changed the name of their city to "San Francisco." So this city was named "Benicia."

Then there is the old state capitol. Indeed, Benicia was California's political seat at one time, for exactly one year, 1853 to 1854. The state capital moved around back in those days, and little Benicia got a turn because of its fine brick City Hall with handsome twin pillars out front. The building has been preserved as it looked in that day, with a candle atop every senator's wood desk, and a brass spittoon right in the middle of the Assembly's chamber.

Benicia has managed to preserve and restore quite a number of its older buildings and you'll find excellent examples of East Coast Federalist, Old-English Edwardian, Spanish-style, and American West architecture. The town grew up so slowly that there isn't one dominant style.

Along with honoring its past, Benicia pitches its main street as a family tourist attraction. And the shady, tree-lined streets, cozy shops, and humid weather make it a pleasant place to meander for a while.

☞ **WHERE TO GO AND WHAT TO DO:**

THE BENICIA CAPITOL, *1st and G Streets, 707-745-3385.*

At the foot of 1st Street is a budding waterfront development on the Sacramento River with wonderful views of the Carquinez Strait and Mount Diablo. It's a great place to fish, read a book, or ponder the mysteries of life.

ARSENAL AND CLOCK TOWER. *If you take Military East Drive (it parallels Interstate 780) to the very end, it'll take you to the Benicia Arsenal and Clock Tower. It's the oldest stone fortress in our part of the country, built in 1859. Also check out the turn-of-the-century mansions nearby.*

HOW TO GET THERE:

From the Bay Area:

Take Interstate 580 to Highway 24 through the Caldecott Tunnel to Interstate 680 north. Follow it up and all the way across the Benicia Bridge, then take the first exit after the bridge which is Interstate 780 west. Take the 2nd Street exit, make a left back under the freeway, and follow the road into town.

port costa

Nestled against the Carquinez Strait, Port Costa is way off the beaten track. You really have to want to go there. Especially because the last three miles are windy, narrow, bumpy, country road. Even if it is a very beautiful country road. Amtrak goes through Port Costa — on its way to somewhere else. In fact, during the week Port Costans pretty well have this town to themselves — all 235 of them.

Then comes the weekend, and Port Costa blooms. The hotels fill up; motorcycles and pickups line the main street. The antique shops and art studios that were shuttered all week suddenly have furniture lining the sidewalk. It's almost a whole different town.

Built in the 1800s, Port Costa was once one of the largest grain ports in the world. The town is surrounded by rich fertile farmland fed by the delta. Huge warehouses near the dock once stored grain. Now, a couple have had their saggy facades rehabilitated and their insides remodeled into artists' lofts and restaurants.

Part of the draw of Port Costa is this cheap, available housing. Apartments here rent for about what you'd pay for garage space in San Francisco. It's beautiful, rural, quiet (most of the time), and there is virtually no crime. Add to that the lure of the water and the long, lazy summer days, and you've got what one resident called "an unfound jewel."

And then she added, "I hope it stays unfound."

☞ WHERE TO GO AND WHAT TO DO:

WAREHOUSE CAFE along Canyon Lake Road is, as its name implies, inside a renovated warehouse. For more expensive tastes there's the BULL VALLEY INN, also along Canyon Lake Road. You can also stay at the Inn which is an old waterfront hotel.

For kids, or grown-ups who still have a lot of kid in them, drive to Port Costa from Crockett along Carquinez Scenic Drive, and look for the sculptures crammed into the yard of an old house on the left side of the road. We particularly like the chrome rocket ship blasting off from behind a fence.

How to get there:

From the Bay Area:

Interstate 80 east to Highway 4 east, to McEwen Road north, which will eventually take you into Port Costa.

locke

THE FIRST WORD THAT COMES TO MIND WHEN YOU VISIT THE LITTLE DELTA TOWN OF LOCKE IS "OLD": OLD WHITEWASHED WOOD HOUSES; FADED OLD STOREFRONTS; A DUSTY, NARROW DOWN-TOWN THAT HASN'T BEEN RESTORED. THE SECOND-FLOOR BALCONIES SAG, AND MANY OF THE SIDEWALKS ARE WOOD PLANKED. LOCKE IS SLOW AND EASY — AND HOT, AND STILL. IT'S AN OLD CHINESE TOWN, AND RESIDENTS SAY A LOT OF THE AIR OF THE OLD CHINESE IS STILL AROUND, HAUNTING THE TOWN.

If any soul really haunts Locke, it must be Tin San Chan. He founded the town in 1912, buying the land from the Locke family. Chinese immigrants had flocked to the delta to get work on the Transcontinental Railroad and the big levy projects, and they felt comfortable here, clustering their simple bungalows behind the town's main street. It wasn't too long before Locke gained fame as the place for a fast time. Opium dens and gambling houses opened up and, this being the time of prohibition, the town was perfect for speakeasies. Chinese and Caucasians, each with their pockets full of gold from the mines, would come here to blow off some steam. You could say Locke was the original R & R resort along the delta.

All that's left of those times is the Dai Loy Gambling House Museum along Main Street, set up as though it's still operating. These days, the houses and bungalows around town are as likely to be occupied by white, middle-class artists as old Chinese. The Chinese who do still live here keep to themselves mostly. Many don't speak English, but they don't need to. Anything important is written in English and Chinese.

The Caucasian artists, on the other hand, speak perfect English but don't especially want to speak to you. They've found their little secret hideaway, and they'd like to keep it. Makes for a very private and fascinating town here on the lazy Sacramento River.

☞ WHERE TO GO AND WHAT TO DO:

DAI LOY GAMBLING HOUSE MUSEUM, *13951 Main Street.*

AL'S PLACE, *also on Main Street, is a "must see." The restaurant serves generously sized meat dishes at reasonable prices. The front of the place is set up as an old-time saloon complete with life-sized murals of a cowboy on his bucking bronco. The ceiling is all covered with dollar bills. It'll cost you a dollar to find out why.*

RIVER ROAD GALLERY, *13944 Main Street. Paintings, sculptures, and other works by local artists.*

HOW TO GET THERE:

From the Bay Area:

Bay Bridge to Interstate 580, then onto Highway 24. Merge onto Interstate 680 north, and take it to Highway 4. Go east on Highway 4, then take Highway 160 north all the way past Walnut Grove and into Locke. This is a long drive, so beware, but it's well worth it.

▨ ▨ ▨

martinez

In the real "olden days," even before the Transcontinental Railroad came through here, the city of Martinez was a way station to dreams of fortune. Gold diggers traveling to the Mother Lode gathered here to catch the ferry across the Carquinez Strait. In this century, Martinez has basked in the glow of a native son who made it very big. His name was Joe DiMaggio, "the Yankee Clipper," who was born in a modest single-story home not far from the tracks.

A lot of World War II veterans remember Martinez as a place where they had a real good time. Martinez was a Navy town, brimming with brothels and bars — 46 bars. If anyone ever counted up the brothels, they didn't write it down. Old-timers say that was the major industry in this town then, with a lot of independent entrepreneurs operating out of basements all over town.

That was then and this is now, and today Martinez has shed its bawdy image. These days it sells itself as a place to raise a family and the hidden secret of Contra Costa County. The weather, the people, the location, and the fishing (sturgeon and bass run during the summer months): All these qualities have held people here despite the lure of bigger cities. This town of 30,000 seems filled with third-, fourth-, and fifth-generation residents who all seem to know each other, and each other's families, and the dusty skeletons in every closet.

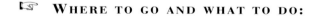

☞ WHERE TO GO AND WHAT TO DO:

Main Street is a very pleasant stroll and takes you to the Martinez train station at the foot of Pine Street.

Also right there is the MARTINEZ REGIONAL SHORELINE, 343 acres of ball fields, a pier, marshes, and bocce ball courts. (This is one of the last remaining rituals of the once large Italian fisherman population here and is still very popular.)

MARTINEZ MUSEUM, *1005 Escobar Street. Open Tuesdays and Thursdays 11:30 am to 3:00 pm. First and third Sundays of each month from 1:00pm to 4:00pm. Perhaps the most spectacular sight in Martinez appears at night. That's when you can see the Shell Oil Refinery lit up like something out of "Close Encounters of the Third Kind." The refinery is on your left as you drive into town.*

How to get there:

From the Bay Area:
Bay Bridge to Interstate 580, then take Highway 24 through the Caldecott Tunnel. Take Interstate 680 north to just before the Benicia Bridge where you'll take the Martinez exit. It's called Waterfront Road. Go left (west) and drive along the river into town.

INDEX